Using Feedback to Improve Learning

Despite feedback's demonstratively positive effects on student performance, research on the specific components of successful feedback practice is in short supply. In *Using Feedback to Improve Learning*, Ruiz-Primo and Brookhart offer critical characteristics of feedback strategies to affirm classroom feedback's positive effect on student learning. The book provides pre- and in-service teachers as well as educational researchers with empirically supported techniques for using feedback as a part of formative assessment in the classroom.

Maria Araceli Ruiz-Primo is Associate Professor in the Graduate School of Education at Stanford University, USA. Her work focuses on assessment of student learning at both large-scale and classroom level, and the study of teachers' assessment practices.

Susan M. Brookhart is Professor Emerita in the School of Education at Duquesne University, USA, and an independent educational consultant based in Helena, Montana. Her interests include the role of both formative and summative classroom assessment in student motivation and achievement, the connection between classroom assessment and large-scale assessment, and grading.

Student Assessment for Educators

Edited by James H. McMillan,
Virginia Commonwealth University, USA

Using Feedback to Improve Learning
Maria Araceli Ruiz-Primo and Susan M. Brookhart

Using Formative Assessment to Enhance Learning, Achievement, and Academic Self-regulation
Heidi L. Andrade and Margaret Heritage

Using Students' Assessment Mistakes and Learning Deficits to Enhance Motivation and Learning
James H. McMillan

Using Feedback to Improve Learning

Maria Araceli Ruiz-Primo
and
Susan M. Brookhart

Routledge
Taylor & Francis Group

NEW YORK AND LONDON

First published 2018
by Routledge
711 Third Avenue, New York, NY 10017

and by Routledge
2 Park Square, Milton Park, Abingdon, Oxon, OX14 4RN

Routledge is an imprint of the Taylor & Francis Group, an informa business

Library of Congress Cataloging-in-Publication Data
A catalog record for this book has been requested

ISBN: 978-1-138-64656-8 (hbk)
ISBN: 978-1-138-64657-5 (pbk)
ISBN: 978-1-315-62750-2 (ebk)

Typeset in Sabon
by Apex CoVantage, LLC

Contents

Preface

Archimedes famously said "Give me a lever long enough and a fulcrum on which to place it, and I shall move the world." He was, of course, extolling the extraordinary power of the lever. In education, feedback is that lever, and what it moves is student learning. Feedback is information, based on evidence in student work that helps students learn and improve. There is ample evidence that, if done well, feedback can do this—and ample evidence that it does not always do so.

The purpose of this book is to present, from a practical and useful perspective, what is known about using feedback to improve student learning. It is written for teacher education students who are learning about feedback, practicing teachers who are interested in improving their feedback to students, and education researchers who study feedback. The book is organized into six chapters. Chapter 1 describes a framework for thinking about formative assessment, of which feedback is a major component. Chapter 2 describes how feedback needs to be rooted in the goals of learning and connected to criteria for that learning. Chapters 3 and 4, together, describe the characteristics of effective feedback, providing a summary of what we know about the feedback message itself, the student and teacher learning that should result, and the next instructional moves that will ensure feedback is used effectively. While most of the book is about feedback from teachers to students, Chapter 5 discusses feedback from other sources, including self- and peer assessment, and feedback from computers. Chapter 6 concludes our book by discussing how feedback may be improved.

Acknowledgments

Dedication from Maria Araceli Ruiz-Primo

To my lovely, supportive, handsome, and always wonderful husband, Dr. Guillermo Solano-Flores. I have learned so much from you, my love. Nobody like you; I simply adore you!

To the Ruiz-Primo family. I wish my mother, Ayaucihuatl, and father, Daniel, were here. They were not only great role models but they also gave me the most wonderful siblings I could ever have—Maria Estela, Daniel, and Maria Elizabeth—who in turn have given me a wonderful and amazing extended family—my in-laws, nieces, and nephews. To all of you with love and admiration. I am so grateful for having you all in my life.

To Dr. Rich Shavelson, my advisor, my academic father, and a role model in every possible way. With gratitude, for your support and friendship all these years. To Patti Shavelson, with appreciation. You have been such a wonderful person with us!

To the teachers who have opened their classrooms' doors and allowed me to learn from them; the colleagues with whom I have had multiple conversations that have shaped my ideas; and the DEMFAP team, whose intense work was critical to concluding some of the investigations mentioned in this book. Special thanks to Dr. Deanna Sands and Dr. Heidi Kroog; we learned a great deal about formative assessment and feedback from working together in DEMFAP.

To Sue Brookhart, with deep appreciation for her friendship, continuous support, and patience. You have always been generous sharing your vast knowledge about classroom and formative assessment. It has been a privilege and honor working with you.

To Jim McMillan. Thank you for the invitation to write this book and for carefully reading and commenting on it.

Dedication from Susan M. Brookhart

There cannot be only one dedication for this book. Without the research and thoughtful scholarship of colleagues in the field, conversations with many practitioners in the field—both K–12 educators and teacher education faculty—and the love and support of family and friends, my participation in this book would not have been possible.

My colleagues in the field are too many to mention, but you can find their names in the reference sections of each chapter. However, I would like to mention two very special colleagues. Maria Araceli Ruiz-Primo, my coauthor, is a valued colleague and friend. Her leadership shaped the book. In particular, she has helped me see the way to fit both feedback comments and next instructional moves into the same framework. Personally, I value her unwavering friendship, her remarkable talent, and the unpretentious and humble—but totally amazing—way she strives to help make learning better for both students in classes and scholars in the field by clearly and carefully sweating the details and seeing the big picture at the same time. James H. McMillan, the editor of this series and the one who asked us to write this book, has also been a valued colleague and unwavering friend over many decades. Together we have seen the field of classroom assessment grow by leaps and bounds. He pushed me to do this book when I was hesitant, and I am glad he did.

Talking with educators in the field has given me insights about where research is needed, how research informs practice and, perhaps most significantly, how conundrums in practice illuminate productive areas for research. Again they are too numerous to name, but I would like to mention the teacher educators at Duquesne University and the administrators and teachers at Armstrong School District, where my colleague and friend Connie Moss and I worked on formative assessment for years. My conversations with Dr. Moss and our work with those K–12 educators helped shape my early understanding of formative assessment in general, and feedback in particular.

Finally, but most importantly, the love and support of my family keeps me going, to do this work and in all other ways. My husband Frank, our daughters Carol and Rachel, and their partners Sean and Amanda are the most wonderful family anyone could have. Together we can do almost anything, and this book is only one example.

1

Formative Assessment and Feedback in the Classroom

The literature on formative assessment has increased substantially in the last 18 years. We can easily find definitions of classroom formative assessment in books and articles; however, frameworks that guide our thinking about formative assessments are rarer.

The goal of this chapter is to introduce you to a framework for thinking about feedback and formative assessment in the classroom. The framework was designed with two essential purposes in mind: (a) to provide a model for thinking about formative assessment and feedback in the classroom, and (b) to help conceptualize feedback in a context broader than oral or written comments in response to student work. This model then provides a way to organize the information presented in each of the subsequent chapters of this book.

We begin with a general discussion of formative assessment and feedback in the classroom that provides a larger context for a description of the major aspects of the framework. This discussion includes an overview of studies that were intended to evaluate the impact of feedback on student learning. We then describe the framework in detail. The chapter closes with a general discussion/overview of the role, purpose, and functions of classroom feedback.

Some Background in Formative Assessment and Feedback

Black and Wiliam (1998) defined formative assessment as "encompassing all those activities undertaken by teachers, and/or by their students, which provide information to be used as feedback to modify the teaching and learning activities in which they are engaged" (p. 7). In this definition feedback is a critical component of the formative assessment process. However, not all definitions of formative assessment include feedback. For example, Bell and Cowie (1999) defined formative assessment as the "process used by teachers and students to recognize and respond to student learning in order to enhance learning during the learning" (p. 198); and Shepard, Hammerness, Darling-Hammond, and Rust (2005) defined it as the "assessment carried out during the instructional process for the purpose of improving teaching or learning" (p. 275). The Assessment Reform Group (nd) in England proposed five elements of assessment. Feedback was included as one of these elements but it was not at the center of what the group called "assessment to improve learning."[1] Leahy, Lyon, Thompson, and Wiliam (2005) identify feedback as a strategy of formative assessment. In a more recent definition of formative assessment the term *feedback* disappears:

> Assessment functions formatively to the extent that evidence about student achievement is elicited, interpreted, and used by teachers, learners, or their peers to make decision about the next steps in instruction that are likely to be better, or better founded, than the decisions they would have made in the absence of that evidence.
>
> (Wiliam, 2011a, p. 43)

Whether the term is part of the definition or not, feedback is regarded as a critical characteristic of formative assessment. Different models have been developed to capture the essence of feedback in the context of formative assessment (e.g., there are models of formative assessment around feedback; see Heritage, 2010). Indeed, to evaluate the impact of formative assessment on improving student learning, researchers mainly cite studies on the effects of feedback.

A substantial literature of books and papers on the topic of feedback and its impact on student learning has accumulated over the last 20 years. Multiple meta-analyses have provided evidence of the effects of feedback on student learning. Feedback has been considered one of the most powerful interventions in education (Hattie, 1999) but also one with the highest variability in its effects (Hattie & Gan, 2011). Most of the recent meta-analyses (e.g., Hattie & Timperley, 2007; Kluger & DeNisi, 1996; Van der Kleij, Feskens, & Eggen, 2015) and reviews (Black & Wiliam, 1998; Shute, 2008) have demonstrated positive effects on student learning outcomes (medium- to large-effect sizes), with a few exceptions showing small effects (Bangert-Drowns, Kulik, Kulik, & Morgan, 1991) and even negative effects (Kluger & DeNisi, 1996; Shute, 2008). Many resources present detailed results of these meta-analyses and reviews (e.g., Black & Wiliam, 1998; Brookhart, 2004, 2007; Mory, 2004; Shute, 2008; Wiliam, 2011a, 2011b).

Despite this accumulated evidence of the effects of feedback, it is difficult to determine clearly what specific types of feedback are effective (Shute, 2008). Furthermore, the overall results of the meta-analyses indicate that not all types of feedback are equally effective. Different issues account for this variability of impact. One of the major issues is that feedback has not been consistently characterized across studies (Ruiz-Primo & Li, 2013a). Feedback can be characterized, for example, by dimensions such as (a) who provides the feedback (e.g., teacher, peer, self, technology-based), (b) the setting in which the feedback is delivered (e.g., individual student, small group, whole class), (c) the role of the student in the feedback event (e.g., provider, receiver), (d) the focus of the feedback (e.g., product, process, or self-regulation for cognitive feedback; or goal orientation or self-efficacy for affective feedback), (e) the artifact used as evidence to provide feedback (e.g., student product, process), (f) the type of feedback provided around the task (e.g., evaluative, descriptive, holistic), (g) how feedback is provided or presented (e.g., written, oral, computerized), or (h) the opportunity provided to respond to the feedback (e.g., revise products). Few studies systematically address these specific characteristics of effective feedback in the classroom and in different disciplines such as science and mathematics education (Ruiz-Primo & Li, 2013a).

A second issue making it difficult to specifically identify effective types of feedback is that some of the meta-analyses grouped fairly dissimilar studies with diverse methodological quality. (e.g., Bennett, 2011; Briggs, Ruiz-Primo, Furtak, Yin, & Shepard, 2012; Ruiz-Primo & Li, 2013a). A third issue relates to the type of empirical evidence provided in many reviews and meta-analyses (Ruiz-Primo & Li, 2013a). The knowledge base about feedback is drawn mainly from studies conducted in laboratories or in artificial classroom environments where learning tasks tend to be minimally meaningful or relevant to learners, and they seldom study long-term feedback effects.

Despite the number of studies reported in the literature, the many models available, and meta-analyses on this topic, feedback practice still is often reported as one of the weakest components of teachers' classroom assessment (Askew, 2000; Black & Wiliam, 1998; Ruiz-Primo & Li, 2004, 2013a, 2013b; Ruiz-Primo & Furtak, 2006, 2007). Even when "teachers provide students with valid and reliable judgments about the quality of their work, improvement does not necessarily follow" (Sadler, 1989, p. 119). Why? What is needed for feedback to have the expected positive effect on students' learning and performance?

Six guiding premises are helpful in examining the role of feedback in formative assessment: (1) *all learning involves interactions* (e.g., Greeno, 1997; Hickey, 2011), (2) *all interactions involve assessments* because assessment is practiced within social interactions (Jordan & Putz, 2004), (3) formative assessment is a complex set of *interrelated assessment practices* (Cowie, 2005), (4) the function of formative assessment and feedback is to improve student learning (e.g., Ramaprasad, 1983; Sadler, 1989; Wiliam & Leahy, 2007), (5) for feedback to have a positive effect on student learning it *must be useful* and *must be used* (Black & Wiliam, 1998; Wiliam & Leahy, 2007), and (6) feedback becomes useful and used when it is *planned in a proactive manner*, rather than treated simply as the information provided to the student (and/or the teacher) in response to something that students did, wrote, said, made, or gestured. These guiding premises shaped the development of the framework for classroom formative assessment we describe in the next section.

A Conceptual Framework to Think About Formative Assessment

The framework we are presenting here is an adaptation of the framework that one of us (Ruiz-Primo, 2010) developed for a project funded by the Institute of Education Sciences (Ruiz-Primo & Sands, 2009), titled *Developing and Evaluating Measures of Formative Assessment Practices* (DEMFAP). One of the purposes of the project was to learn more about how formative assessment was implemented on an everyday basis in mathematics and science classrooms. The reason we adopt and adapt the framework is because we believe it can help you understand the different aspects involved in implementing quality formative assessment, which in turn can lead to applying feedback in useful ways to improve students' learning.

The proposed framework is based on theoretical perspectives, research, and practitioner knowledge. It brings together concepts that originated in the cognitive sciences, ideas about a sociocultural perspective of learning, and what research and practitioners have identified as important issues related to assessment *for* learning. The framework is based on the four pillars of the DEMFAP framework: *assessment cycles or episodes*, the *formality of assessment practices*, the *teachers' and the students' roles* at each step of the assessment cycle, and the *context* in which these activities occur. Figure 1.1 presents the dimensions of the formative assessment framework.

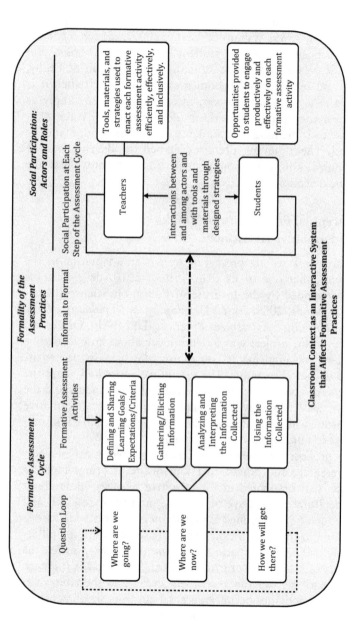

Figure 1.1 Formative Assessment Framework

Adapted from the DEMFAP framework; Ruiz-Primo (2010).

Theoretical Perspectives

Cognitive Perspective on Learning

There are two essential cognitive components to consider when thinking about formative assessment: cognition and regulation.

COGNITION

Cognition refers to the thinking activities that students use to process content and achieve learning outcomes. Teachers must keep student thinking in mind when they define the learning goals, select strategies to elicit information from students, analyze and interpret what they find, and respond to students. "Awareness of the role of cognitive process in assessment enables educators to obtain the maximum benefit from assessment activities and information" (Solano-Flores, 2016, p. 37). If you are aware of students' cognitive processes, you will appreciate the importance of selecting or designing questions and tasks for students. How questions are posed will determine the cognitive processes most likely to be elicited from students. The quality of the learning activities in which students engage will determine the quality of the learning outcomes they eventually achieve (Vermunt & Verloop, 1999).

Different taxonomies tap different cognitive processing activities. The taxonomy created by Bloom and his colleagues (Bloom, 1956; Bloom, Engelhart, Furst, Hill, & Krathwohl, 1956) is the most familiar in the field. Other taxonomies of cognitive processes exist. For example, Porter (2002) offers a classification of performance goals in mathematics and provides a language that is frequently associated with performance goals. An instance of a performance goal is *communicate understanding of concepts*. Porter proposes the following language to translate this learning goal: communicate mathematical ideas, use representations to model mathematical ideas, explain findings and results from statistical analyses, or explain reasoning. Webb (2007) provides a classification for judging curriculum standards and their alignment with assessments using the idea of *depth of knowledge*; from Level 1, which involves recalling information such as fact or performing a simple algorithm, to Level 4, which requires complex reasoning, planning, and developing over an extended period of time. Ritchhart, Church, and Morrison (2011) propose a list of high-leverage *thinking moves* that will engage students in deep understanding such as building explanations and interpretations, or reasoning with evidence, or making connections. Li, Ruiz-Primo, and Shavelson (2006) have proposed four interdependent types of knowledge that result from learning within a content domain: *Declarative knowledge*—Knowing that, *Procedural knowledge*—Knowing how, *Schematic knowledge*—Knowing why, and *Strategic knowledge*—Knowing when, where, and how to apply knowledge. The Third International Mathematics and Science Study (TIMSS, 2003) proposed three cognitive domains in science (factual knowledge, conceptual understanding, reasoning and analysis) and four in mathematics (knowing facts and procedures, using concepts, solving routine problems, and reasoning). The Programme for International Student Assessment (PISA) framework for assessing students (Organisation for Economic Co-operation and Development, 2013) also provides some categories related to cognitive demands (e.g., students recognize, offer, and evaluate explanations for a range of natural and technological phenomena). Whatever the taxonomy being used, what matters is that it reflects the type of cognitive processes (thinking) you want students to use. Once you are clear on what these thinking processes are, you need to value and promote them in the classroom during both instruction and assessment.

REGULATION

Another concept addressed in the framework is *regulation* and its critical role in learning. "All theories of learning propose a mechanism of regulation . . . [] . . . equilibrium in Piaget's constructivism, feedback devices in cognitive models, and social mediation in sociocultural and social constructivist approaches" (Allal, 2010, p. 348). The idea is that students regulate their learning process when they are involved in *cognitive* processing activities, in *affective* activities to cope with emotions during learning, and *metacognitive* activities to exercise control over the cognitive and affective activities to achieve the learning goals (Vermunt & Verloop, 1999).

Formative assessment plays a "pervasive role in the regulation of learning when it is integrated from the beginning in each teaching and learning activity" (Allal, 2010, p. 350). Feedback is a critical element at every stage of the regulation process: goal setting/orienting/planning, monitoring progress toward the goal, interpreting results from monitoring to adjust actions, and evaluating whether the learning process has proceeded as expected and the learning goal has been achieved (Allal, 2010, 2011; Vermunt & Verloop, 1999). Formative assessment activities and the activation of regulation are closely linked since one fosters or constrains the other (e.g., clarity about what learning is being pursued triggers monitoring progress toward the goal, or the quality of the feedback provided does not help the student to monitor her own actions).

This reflexive relationship, as it is named by Allal (2011), has led to interpreting assessment as a *co-regulation process* (Allal, 2010, 2011; Andrade & Brookhart, 2016), in which student learning is seen as reflecting the joint influence of the *individual* regulation process (self-regulation) and the *social* regulation process (external regulation). Social regulation results from interactive guidance (e.g., teacher-student interactions, student-student interactions, or teacher-classroom interactions) and is influenced by the learning environment (e.g., instructional tasks, instructional materials, the culture of the classroom).

The individual and social dimensions of regulation of learning have important implications for assessment:

1. Assessment should be embedded in teaching and learning (Allal, 2010; Vermunt & Verloop, 1999), since most of what teachers and students do in the classroom offers potential opportunities for assessing in ways that promote the regulation of learning.
2. Feedback should function as a mechanism of co- and self-regulation that allows the student to progress toward the learning goal and toward becoming an independent learner.

3. Students should be involved in the assessment process in a way that stimulates their use of strategies for regulating their cognition, meta-cognition, and affect.
4. The tools that are used in the classroom (e.g., instructional tasks) should be designed to allow for student self-regulation.
5. Teachers should create a learning environment that encourages students' self-regulation and gives students appropriate external regulation as they learn.

Formative feedback should not be limited to adapting the teaching and learning activities to the students' needs (one form of regulation), but also to help students monitor their own strengths and weaknesses as reflected in their performances, so "that aspects associated with success or high quality can be recognized and reinforced, and unsatisfactory aspects modified or improved" (Sadler, 1989, p. 121).

Sociocultural Perspective on Learning

The framework relies on the idea that cognitive processes are shaped by society and do not occur in isolation. This sociocultural approach to learning views knowledge as socially constructed and context-dependent. Everyday classroom practices define the types of teacher and student interactions that will occur in the course of daily instruction and assessment. These practices shape how students come to see themselves as learners and knowers of a subject (Brown & Harris, 2016; Cowie, 2005; Gipps, 1999). The classroom is an interactive system that includes "individual participants, interacting with each other and with materials and representational systems" (Greeno, 1997).

Dimensions of Formative Assessment

Formative Assessment as a Cycle

The *formative assessment cycle* dimension relies on a merger of critical ideas related to feedback. For example, Ramaprasad (1983) makes important points about feedback as a system-control function. First, feedback applies not only to outcomes (or students' responses), it can also focus on any aspect of the process of producing an outcome (e.g., effort put on a task). Second, the necessary conditions for feedback include a reference level of performance, knowledge about the actual level, and a mechanism for comparing the reference and the actual level. Third, the definition of feedback is based on its effect rather than its content—information qualifies as feedback only *if* the information resulting from the comparison of the reference and the actual level is used to alter the gap between the two levels.

The work of Ramaprasad (1983) draws attention to three instructional processes proposed by Sadler (1989), which have been the basis for the assessment cycle. According to Sadler (1989) there are three conditions for improvement. For students to be in control during the production of their responses, they need to (a) understand what constitutes the goal or quality level being pursued or aimed for, (b) compare the actual level of performance with criteria, and (c) engage in actions that will lead to some closure of the gap between where they are and where they should be. Sadler (1989) distinguishes between feedback and self-monitoring according to the source of the evaluative information. That is, feedback is external to the student, and self-monitoring is generated by the student. Formative assessment should help students move from using feedback to self-monitoring. Wiliam and Leahy (2007) redefined these conditions as instructional processes: where students are going, where the students are in their learning, and what needs to be done to help students close the gap. They expressed these instructional processes as questions: where is the learner going?; where is the learner right now?; and how does the learner get there (to achieve the learning goal)? Others have posed the same questions in different ways (e.g., Hattie & Timperley, 2007). In the DEMFAP framework the questions were posed in a way that represents student participation in the assessment process: where are *we* going?; where are *we* now?; and how will *we* get there?

Finally, Bell and Cowie (2001) observed a formative assessment cycle in their study of science classrooms. This cycle includes eliciting information, interpreting information, and acting on/using the information collected with a purpose. Bell and Cowie (2001) offer two types of assessment cycles, planned and interactive, both of which they observed during student-teacher interactions. They use different terms depending on the type of cycle. The planned cycle uses eliciting, interpreting, and acting with a purpose at the center. The interactive cycle is made up of noticing, recognizing, and responding with a purpose at the center. Formative assessment represents the interplay between the planned and the interactive cycles. The framework uses clarifying learning goals, expectations, and criteria rather than purpose. This aspect taps the importance of establishing where the students are going.

The framework aligns the aspects proposed by Bell and Cowie with the questions suggested in the work by Ramaprasad and Sadler, in the left part of Figure 1.1. The idea of assessment as a cyclical (iterative) process is represented with arrows that form a loop.

Formality in Formative Assessment

Not every researcher in this area distinguishes between informal and formal formative assessment (e.g., Heritage, 2010, 2013; Wiliam, 2011a). From our perspective, however, the distinction is important because of its implications for what classroom teachers do in their everyday practices. Formality refers to the degree of planning involved in the enactment of formative assessment and feedback. Rather than setting up a dichotomous model of formative assessment as proposed by Bell and Cowie (2001), the framework incorporates the idea of a continuum between what has been called *informal* formative assessment and *formal* formative assessment (Ruiz-Primo & Furtak, 2006, 2007; Ruiz-Primo, Furtak, Ayala, Yin, & Shavelson, 2010; Shavelson, Yin, Furtak, Ruiz-Primo, & Ayala, 2008). The degree to which the assessment event is planned determines its formality (Ruiz-Primo, 2010). The framework then considers the fact that formative assessment cycles be implemented in several ways with varying levels of formality. This variation is represented as a continuum at the center of Figure 1.1 and makes it possible for you to think about formative assessment not only as process that requires embedded assessment. Rather, any dialogue that happens in the classroom, any learning activity or instructional resource (e.g., exit tickets, notebooks), as well as very formal assessment tasks (e.g., quizzes or tests) are all opportunities of formative assessment and, therefore, of feedback (Bell & Cowie, 2001; Ruiz-Primo & Furtak, 2006, 2007).

While informal formative assessment (IFA) provides the opportunity to address students' individual needs, formal formative assessment (FFA) is a way for the teacher to determine where larger groups of students are in their learning. In FFA, we are more likely to collect information from all or almost all the students. In contrast, with IFA, every activity that happens in the classroom offers a *potential* opportunity to gather information about students' learning. Sometimes this opportunity comes from one student and the question she asks, sometimes from the conversation students are having while working in small groups, or sometimes from a whole-class discussion. In any of these situations, however, it is not likely that the teacher can gather information from all of the students, as it is characteristic of FFA.

Social Participation: Teachers' and Students' Roles

"Social participation" refers to teachers' and students' roles in a formative assessment event. Teachers and students are viewed as actors whose roles are shaped by the specific formative assessment practice being implemented and by the activity being conducted (Ruiz-Primo, 2010). The formative assessment actors are represented in the right side of Figure 1.1. This dimension takes into account the different settings in which the assessment activity cycle can take place, for example, one-on-one, pairs, small groups, or whole-class activity.

As in the DEFMAP framework (Ruiz-Primo, 2010), we incorporate the idea of *sampling* in any formative assessment event. Sampling "is the process through which a proportion of a whole is examined with the intent to make generalizations about the characteristics of a population or universe (the whole) based on the characteristics of the sample" (Solano-Flores, 2016, p. 12). This concept is especially important when we think about informal formative assessment. By definition, information obtained informally is sampled (e.g., from one student working individually or selected from among the whole group, a pair of students, or a small group). Conclusions based on responses of just one or two students may not accurately reflect students' learning in the class as a whole. Asking questions of students can be seen as drawing a sample, as well. The issue is whether a generalization based on selected student answers is appropriate and valid. The idea of sampling has helped us observe some bias in teachers' questioning. For example, asking the same students (those likely to know the appropriate response) or never calling on students who tend to be reticent for different reasons (e.g., English language learners) could lead to the wrong conclusions (e.g., everybody is understanding).

Context

The context dimension of the framework focuses on teachers' and students' activities and the social organization within which the assessment activity cycle takes place (e.g., one-on-one, pairs, small groups, or whole class). In Figure 1.1 context is represented by the shaded rectangle that encompasses the other dimensions. We acknowledge that classrooms are communities guided by norms, beliefs, practices, tools, and artifacts. These factors and elements together influence how formative assessment is implemented and also shaped.

Rethinking Feedback: Role, Purpose, and Function

The framework emphasizes three characteristics. First, students should not be seen solely as recipients of the feedback. They are also participants in formative feedback activities (e.g., clarifying learning goals or success criteria), and they can be providers and developers of actions to be followed. Second, in a classroom context, the definition of feedback should extend beyond oral or written comments to students' work. In a regular classroom and on the everyday basis, there is a blurred distinction between feedback and instruction (Heritage, 2010). Therefore, we believe it is important to think about two types of feedback: comments (oral or written) and instructional moves (e.g., modeling or conducting demonstrations). Both comments and instructional moves are intended to modify students' thinking or behavior with the purpose of improving learning. Third, a feedback episode is not a discrete activity; rather, it combines looking for evidence of students' learning during ongoing interactions and communicating to students in the on-the-fly situation (Moss, 2008; Ruiz-Primo, 2011; Ruiz-Primo & Furtak, 2006, 2007).

Ruiz-Primo and Li (2013a) discussed the role of feedback in formative assessment events based on assertions generally accepted by theorists and researchers. In their view, formative assessment and feedback should:

- *Be seen and treated as a process* strongly guided by the learning goal(s) of the teacher and students. The formative role of feedback cannot be fully understood without connecting it to the targeted learning goal and comparing the expected level with the achieved level as defined by criteria of success (Ramaprasad, 1983; Sadler, 1989). Feedback should be based on well-articulated evidence of learning and/or criteria to be confident that the intended goals have been met. Formative assessment and feedback should include the instructional process of comparing the current or actual level of student performance with the success criteria and communicate assessment information to improve student learning to reduce or close the gap (Nichols, Meyers, & Burling, 2009; Shepard, 2009). Finally, the recipient should use the information. This is a difficult step (Hickey, 2011).

- *Actively involve students in the process* by including them in (a) defining the evidence of learning and/or success criteria (or goal, or reference level) being targeted, (b) comparing the current or actual level of performance with the evidence or the criteria for success, and (c) using assessment information to improve their own learning to reduce the gap. A critical aspect of formative assessment is that both students and teachers participate in generating and using the assessment information (Brookhart, 2009, 2012; Brookhart, Moss, & Long, 2009).

Also, students can talk with their teacher and collaboratively determine what type of feedback is more useful for the students (e.g., provide examples or provide criteria or both). All of these practices entail the use of peer and self-feedback.

- *Be considered as an instructional scaffold* that goes beyond written or oral comments. Formative feedback can involve any verbal exchange (conversation, dialogue, discussion), modeling, demonstrations, cues, or hints that can support learning, such as how a teacher responds to a student's incorrect answer with a probing question (Askew & Lodge, 2000; Heritage, 2010; Ruiz-Primo & Furtak, 2006, 2007). However, we need to learn more about nonverbal strategies such as gestures or body language; instructional actions such as demonstrating, modeling, or conferring; and vicarious feedback (e.g., whole-class or small-group discussions that other students can listen to and learn from).

- *Be specifically designed to improve learning outcomes* (e.g., deepening conceptual understanding) and *processes* (e.g., reflecting on one's learning and learning strategies, or making new connections to what has been learned; see Askew & Lodge, 2000). When feedback is directed at improving learning outcomes, its content will focus on reducing the difference between a current understanding or performance level and what is expected. It will also seek to improve students' learning strategies, helping the students to monitor their own learning and strengthening their belief in their ability to take charge of their own learning. As such, feedback should further *focus on self-regulation*. This focus should contain information that is under the students' control (e.g., effort, ways to monitor or check work, strategies to set up a work plan), in contrast to evaluating an individual's ability or personality.

- *Ensure use and usefulness of formative assessment by making feedback accessible and practical.* Feedback is appropriate if it is (a) *helpful* by letting the students know what to do next and what future actions to expect (Wiliam, 2011a), (b) *precise* by identifying what was right or wrong in their responses and describing the ways in which something was right or wrong (Gipps, McCallum, & Hargreaves, 2000; Tunstall & Gipps,

1996; Wiliam, 2011a), and (c) *at the right level* for the students (Carnell, 2000). Students should have an opportunity to act on feedback from others (teachers, peers) and plan next steps to ensure their own continued learning (e.g., What could make this a better table? Shall I sort the data based on the first column or the second?; Gipps, McCallum, & Hargreaves, 2000). When students assess themselves, they should construct their own feedback and think about how to use the information learned from self-assessment to improve their performance.

- *Consider different sources of information* about students' learning and understanding from highly formal (e.g., unit tests, filling in a handout, completing an investigation report) to very informal (e.g., questions, comments, observations, conversations between students) (Bell & Cowie, 2001; Ruiz-Primo, 2010; Ruiz-Primo & Furtak, 2006, 2007; Ruiz-Primo et al., 2010; Shavelson et al., 2008).

Closing Comments

In this chapter we have presented feedback as more than simply limited information given to students in response to their answers to various classroom learning activities. We have described a conceptual framework derived from research. The framework proposed *formative assessment cycles* as a critical concept for contextualizing feedback as part of four activities: (a) clarifying learning goals (expectations and/or criteria), (b) collecting information, (c) analyzing and interpreting information, and (d) acting on/using the information collected to move students closer to the learning goals and supporting the necessary steps. We believe the framework will help you to think more deeply and critically about implementation issues related to feedback, and to study feedback in the classroom with increased precision and understanding.

Note

1 The five elements proposed by the Assessment Reform Group in England are: (1) provision of effective feedback, (2) active involvement

of students in their own learning, (3) adjustment of teaching to take into account the results of assessments, (4) recognition of the profound influence that assessment has on motivation, and (5) the need for students to be able to assess themselves and understand how to improve.

References

Allal, L. (2010). Assessment and the regulation of learning. In E. B. P. Peterson (Ed.), *International encyclopedia of education* (Vol. 3, pp. 348–352). Oxford: Elsevier.

Allal, L. (2011). Pedagogy, didactics and the co-regulation of learning: A perspective from the French-language world of educational research. *Research Papers in Education*, 26(3), 329–336.

Andrade, H., & Brookhart, S. (2016). Classroom assessment as the co-regulation of learning. Paper under review.

Askew, S. (2000). *Feedback for learning*. London: Routledge Falmer.

Askew, S., & Lodge, S. (2000). Gifts, ping-pong and loops—linking feedback and learning. In S. Askew (Ed.), *Feedback for learning* (pp. 17–32). New York, NY: Routledge.

Bangert-Drowns, R. L., Kulik, C-L., Kulik, J. A., & Morgan, M. T. (1991). The instructional effect of feedback in test-like events. *Review of Educational Research*, 61(2), 213–238.

Bell, B., & Cowie, B. (1999). *Researching formative assessment*. In J. Loughran (Ed.), *Researching teaching: Methodologies and practices for understanding pedagogy* (pp. 198–214). London: Falmer Press.

Bell, B., & Cowie, B. (2001). *Formative assessment and science education*. Dordrecht, The Netherlands: Kluwer.

Bennett, R. E. (2011). Formative assessment: A critical review. *Assessment in Education: Principles, Policy & Practice*, 18(1), 5–25.

Black, P., & Wiliam, D. (1998). Assessment and classroom learning. *Assessment in Education: Principles, Policy, & Practice*, 5(1), 7–74.

Bloom, B. S. (1956). *Taxonomy of educational objectives: The classification of educational goals. Handbook 1: Cognitive domain*. London, WI: Longmans, Green & Co. Ltd.

Bloom, B. S., Engelhart, M. D., Furst, E. J., Hill., W. H., & Krathwohl, D. R. (Eds.). (1956). *Taxonomy of educational objectives: The classification of educational goals. Handbook 1: Cognitive domain*. London, WI: Longmans, Green & Co. Ltd.

Briggs, D., Ruiz-Primo, M. A., Furtak, E., Yin, Y., & Shepard, L. (2012). Meta-analytic methodology and inferences about the efficacy of formative assessment. *Educational Measurement: Issues and Practices*, *31*(4), 13–17.

Brookhart, S. (2004). Classroom assessment: Tensions and intersections in theory and practice. *Teachers College Record*, *106*(3), 429–458.

Brookhart, S. (2007). Expanding views about formative classroom assessment: A review of the literature. In J. H. McMillan (Ed.), *Formative classroom assessment: Theory into practice* (pp. 43–62). New York: Teachers College Press.

Brookhart, S. (2009). *Exploring formative assessment*. Alexandria, VA: ASCD.

Brookhart, S. (2012). Preventing feedback fizzle. *Educational Leadership*, *70*(1), 25–29.

Brookhart, S., Moss, C. M., & Long, B. A. (2009). Promoting student ownership of learning through high-impact formative assessment practices. *Journal of Multidisciplinary Evaluation*, *6*(12), 52–67.

Brown, G. T. L., & Harris, L. R. (Eds.). (2016). *Handbook of human and social conditions in assessment*. New York, NY: Routledge.

Carnell, E. (2000). Dialogue, discussion and feedback—views of secondary school students on how others help their learning. In S. Askew (Ed.), *Feedback for learning* (pp. 56–69). New York, NY: Routledge.

Cowie, B. (2005). Student commentary on classroom assessment in science: A sociocultural interpretation. *International Journal of Science Education*, *27*(2), 199–214.

Gipps, C. (1999). Socio-cultural aspects of assessment. *Review of Educational Research*, *24*, 355–392.

Gipps, C., McCallum, B., & Hargreaves, E. (2000). *What makes a good primary school teacher: Expert classroom strategies*. London: Falmer.

Greeno, J. G. (1997). On claims that answer the wrong questions. *Educational Researcher*, *26*(1), 5–17.

Hattie, J. (1999, August). *Influences on student learning*. Inaugural lecture: Professor of education, University of Auckland. Retrieved from www.arts.auckland.ac.nz/staff/index.cfm?P=5049

Hattie, J. & Gan, M. (2011). Instruction based on feedback. In R. E. Mayer & P. A. Alexander (Eds.), *Handbook of research on learning and instruction* (pp. 249–271). New York, NY: Routledge, Taylor & Francis Group.

Hattie, J., & Timperley, H. (2007). The power of feedback. *Review of Educational Research*, *77*(1), 81–112.

Heritage, M. (2010). *Formative assessment: Making it happen in the classroom*. Thousand Oaks, CA: Corwin.

Heritage, M. (2013). *Formative assessment in practice: A process of inquiry and action*. Cambridge, MA: Harvard Education Press.

Hickey, D. (2011). Commentary: A gentle critique of formative assessment and a participatory alternative. In P. E. Noyce & D. T. Hickey (Eds.), *New frontiers in formative assessment* (pp. 207–222). Cambridge, MA: Harvard Education Press.

Jordan, B., & Putz, P. (2004). Assessment as practice: Notes on measures, tests, and targets. *Human Organization, 63*, 346–358.

Kluger, A. N., & DeNisi, A. (1996). The effects of feedback interventions on performance: A historical review, a meta-analysis, and a preliminary feedback intervention theory. *Psychological Bulletin, 119*, 254–284.

Leahy, S., Lyon, C., Thompson, M., & Wiliam, D. (2005). Classroom assessment: Minute by minute, day by day. *Educational Leadership, 63*(3), 19–24.

Li, M., Ruiz-Primo, M. A., & Shavelson, R. J. (2006). Towards a science achievement framework: The case of TIMSS 1999. In S. Howie & T. Plomp (Eds.), *Contexts of learning mathematics and science: Lessons learned from TIMSS* (pp. 291–311). London: Routledge.

Mory, E. H. (2004). Feedback research revisited. In D. Jonassen (Ed.), *Handbook of research on educational communications and technology* (pp. 745–783). Mahwah, NJ: Lawrence Erlbaum.

Moss, P. A. (2008). Sociocultural implications for the practice of assessment I: Classroom assessment. In P. A. Moss, D. Pullin, J. P. Gee, E. H. Haertel, & L. J. Young (Eds.), *Assessment, equity, and opportunity to learn* (pp. 222–258). New York: Cambridge University Press.

Nichols, P. D., Meyers, J. L., & Burling, K. S. (2009). A framework for evaluating and planning assessments intended to improve. *Educational Measurement: Issues and Practice, 28*(3), 14–23.

Organisation for Economic Co-operation and Development. (2013). Programme for International Student Assessment—PISA 2015. Draft Science Framework. February 28, 2016, from www.oecd.org/pisa/pisaproducts/Draft%20PISA%202015%20Science%20Framework%20.pdf

Porter, A. C. (2002). Measuring the content instruction: Uses in research and practice. *Educational Researcher, 31*(7), 3–14.

Ramaprasad, A. (1983). On the definition of feedback. *Behavioral Science, 28*, 4–13.

Ritchhart, R., Church, M., & Morrison, K. (2011). *Making thinking visible: How to promote engagement, understanding, and independence for all learners*. San Francisco, CA: Jossey-Bass.

Ruiz-Primo, M. A. (2010). *Developing and Evaluating Measures of Formative Assessment Practice (DEMFAP) theoretical and methodological approach*. Internal manuscript. University of Colorado Denver. Denver, CO: Laboratory of Educational Assessment, Research, and Innovation (LEARN).

Ruiz-Primo, M. A. (2011). Informal formative assessment: The role of instructional dialogues in assessing students' learning. Special Issue in Assessment *for* Learning *Studies in Educational Evaluation*, *37*(1), 15–24.

Ruiz-Primo, M. A., & Furtak, E. M. (2006). Informal formative assessment and scientific inquiry: Exploring teachers' practices and student learning. *Educational Assessment*, *11*(3–4), 205–235.

Ruiz-Primo, M. A., & Furtak, E. M. (2007). Exploring teachers' informal formative assessment practices and students' understanding in the context of scientific inquiry. *Journal of Research in Science Teaching*, *44*(1), 57–84.

Ruiz-Primo, M. A., Furtak, E., Ayala, C., Yin, Y., & Shavelson. R. J. (2010). Formative assessment, motivation, and science learning. In G. J., Cizek, & H. Andrade (Eds.), *Handbook of formative assessment* (pp. 139–158). New York, NY: Routledge, Taylor & Francis Group.

Ruiz-Primo, M. A., & Li, M. (2004). On the use of students' science notebooks as an assessment tool. *Studies in Educational Evaluation*, *30*, 61–85.

Ruiz-Primo, M. A., & Li, M. (2013a). Examining formative feedback in the classroom context: New research perspectives. In J. H. McMillan (Ed.), *Handbook on research on classroom assessment* (pp. 215–232). Los Angeles: Sage.

Ruiz-Primo, M. A., & Li, M. (2013b). Analyzing teachers' feedback practices in response to students' work in science classrooms. Special Issue on Using Evidence to Take Action: Strategies Teachers Use to Deconstruct Student Work. *Applied Measurement in Education*, *26*(3), 163–175.

Ruiz-Primo, M. A., & Sands, D. (2009). *Developing and Evaluating Measures of Formative Assessment Practices (DEMFAP)*. Proposal submitted and awarded to the Institute of Education Sciences. Cognition and Student Learning. Award ID: R305A100571.

Sadler, D. R. (1989). Formative assessment and the design of instructional systems. *Instructional Science*, *18*, 119–144.

Shavelson, R. J., Yin, Y., Furtak, E. M., Ruiz-Primo, M. A., & Ayala, C. (2008). On the role and impact of formative assessment on science inquiry teaching and learning. In J. Coffey, R. Douglas, & C. Stearns (Eds.), *Assessing science learning: Perspectives from research and practice* (pp. 21–36). Arlington, VA: National Science Teachers Association Press.

Shepard, L. (2009). Commentary: Evaluating the validity of formative and interim assessment. *Educational Measurement: Issues and Practice*, 28(3), 32–37.

Shepard, L., Hammerness, K., Darling-Hammond, L., & Rust, F. (2005). Assessment. In L. Darling-Hammond & J. Bransford (Eds.), *Preparing teachers for a changing world: What teachers should learn and be able to do* (pp. 275–326). San Francisco: Jossey-Bass.

Shute, V. J. (2008). Focus on formative feedback. *Review of Educational Research*, 78(1), 153–189.

Solano-Flores, G. (2016). *Assessing English language learners: Theory and practice*. New York, NY: Routledge.

Third International Mathematics and Science Study. (2003). *TIMSS assessment framework and specification 2003*. International Association for the Evaluation of Educational Achievement (IEA). Lynch School of Education, Boston College. Chestnut Hill, MA: Boston College.

Tunstall, P., & Gipps, C. (1996). Teacher feedback to young children in formative assessment: A typology. *British Educational Research Journal*, 22(4), 389–404.

Van der Kleij, F. M., Feskens, R. C. W., & Eggen, T. J. H. M. (2015). Effects of feedback in a computer-based learning environment on students' learning outcomes: A meta-analysis. *Review of Educational Research*, 85(4), 475–511.

Vermunt, J. D., & Verloop, N. (1999). Congruence and friction between learning and teaching. *Learning and Instruction*, 4(9), 257–280.

Webb, N. L. (2007). Issues related to judging the alignment of curriculum standards and assessments. *Applied Measurement in Education*, 20(1), 7–25.

Wiliam, D. (2011a). *Embedded formative assessment*. Bloomington, IN: Solution Tree Press.

Wiliam, D. (2011b). What is assessment for learning. *Studies in Educational Evaluation*, 37(1), 3–14.

Wiliam, D., & Leahy, S. (2007). A theoretical foundation for formative assessment. In J. H. McMillan (Ed.), *Formative classroom assessment: Theory into practice* (pp. 29–42). New York, NY: Teachers College Press.

2

Feedback, Goals of Learning, and Criteria for Success

The theme of this chapter is that feedback about learning should be based on goals for learning and the criteria for success that are shared between teachers and students. Learning goals and success criteria are two aspects of the same concept. Both show students where they should focus their learning efforts. It is very important for feedback to be based on success criteria, those qualities that students and teachers look for in student work to answer the question of quality and of progress toward the learning goal. Theorists of formative assessment argue that sharing the criteria is part of sharing the learning target (Sadler, 1989; Wiliam, 2010). "Where are we going?" (question 1) asks about the learning goal, and "How will we know?" asks about the success criteria. The practical literature about formative assessment, too, stresses that a learning target without success criteria is incomplete and unlikely to realize effective use of formative assessment evidence or feedback (Heritage, 2010; Moss & Brookhart, 2012).

In this chapter, we first define and describe learning goals and criteria for success and present research evidence that when students have learning goals and clear criteria, feedback and self-assessment are more effective, and learning and motivation increase. Then we discuss the idea that teachers, as well as students, need to learn from feedback episodes. Teachers need to learn what students are thinking, and students need to learn the status of their learning and their next steps.

Learning Goals

Learning goals are statements about the things we intend for students to learn. Meaningful learning goals should challenge students' thinking and significantly extend their capabilities and understandings (Eraut, 1997). Such goals incorporate principled understandings that typically form the foundation for more advanced learning because of their higher explanatory power and flexible application (Brown, Kane, & Echols, 1986). These kinds of learning goals should make a difference in how students think and perform after they have learned something new.

Learning goals are written at different grain sizes. Sometimes you will hear the very general catchphrase "what students will know and be able to do." In the United States, for example, state education departments have state standards that are written at a high level of generality (e.g., "Demonstrate understanding of grade-level informational text"). School districts and schools usually have curriculum documents in each subject that have goals for units of instruction derived from those standards (e.g., "Summarize the main idea in one-paragraph informational text, and explain how the idea is supported by key details"). Individual lessons or groups of lessons in the unit may be driven by instructional objectives at a smaller grain size (e.g., "The student will find details that support the main idea in one-paragraph informational texts where the main idea is stated explicitly"). The formative assessment cycle within individual lessons is based on lesson-sized, student-friendly learning targets (e.g., "I can find the main idea in [this text] and show how key details support it").

The most powerful formative learning cycles are based on short- and medium-cycle learning goals (Wiliam, 2010). Students' progress toward individual lessons' learning targets is fed with minute-to-minute formative feedback such as comments on students' class work. In terms of the Framework for Formative Assessment (Chapter 1), feedback on short-cycle, in-class learning targets is usually informal. Students and teachers participate, and either may initiate. Students' progress toward medium-cycle learning goals (e.g., unit goals or objectives that span several lessons) is often fed with feedback on more formal formative assessment evidence, for example from quizzes or drafts of assignments (Wiliam, 2016).

The importance of understanding the learning goals, by you first, and then by your students, is a foundational principle of formative assessment (Sadler, 1989). If students are not clear about what they are supposed to be learning and how they will know, they are left doing an assignment simply because a teacher asked them to. In that case, students will experience feedback as just more teacher directions—or possibly teacher coaching for how to get a good grade. For these students, self-assessment only occurs in the most general sense ("Does this seem like good work?") or regarding surface-level features ("Is this neat? Is it long enough?").

However, if students are active participants in a formative feedback episode, then both the students and the teacher are working within a cycle bounded by the three important guiding questions from Chapter 1: Where are we going? Where are we? How will we get there? When teachers explain learning goals, give a meaningful rationale, and reveal what competency or mastery looks like (Bransford, Brown, & Cocking, 2000; Ryan & Deci, 2000), students are better able to aim for mastery (Hattie & Timperley, 2007; Sadler, 1989). These targets should be arranged in a learning trajectory (Sztajn, Confrey, Wilson, & Edgington, 2012).

Clear learning goals facilitate your accomplishment of a number of important practices that allow you to (a) share the goals, expectations, and criteria with the students in ways that make it clear for them what they are aiming for (Sadler, 1989); (b) help students recognize and understand the gap between those goals and where they are and what they need to do (Sadler, 1989); (c) determine what information you need to collect; (d) be more clear about the most appropriate strategies for gathering the information; (e) recognize the kind of evidence students should pay attention to and the criteria they should use to determine whether learning is taking place; and (f) facilitate or provide direct feedback that is meaningful for students.

Some research into actual teaching practice has shown that just telling students what their learning target is supposed to be, or posting a list of criteria on the board, does not really amount to sharing learning targets and criteria effectively. The learning targets and criteria need to be an integral part of, and implemented throughout, the whole lesson. Teachers who are effective at formative assessment share learning targets and criteria for success with students early and often in a lesson. Moss, Brookhart, and Long (2013) asked administrators in a large school district to identify one teacher who was accomplished in formative assessment, one who was medium, and one teacher who was not very accomplished in formative assessment. The administrators observed teachers in their classrooms. In this district, almost every teacher observed shared learning targets and success criteria orally, no matter what their skill level at formative assessment. Accomplished teachers, however, used more than one mode (sharing learning targets orally, in writing, via displays, or via demonstrations and modeling). Similarly, many teachers shared learning targets and criteria prior to instruction, though most of the accomplished teachers also shared learning targets and criteria for success before, during, and at the conclusion of instruction.

Ruiz-Primo and Kroog (2015) and Kroog and Ruiz-Primo (2015) investigated how teachers clarified learning goals in two studies that were part of the DEMFAP project. In both studies the purpose was to learn how the learning goals were introduced to students and how students participated in this formative assessment activity. In the first study, Ruiz-Primo and Kroog identified eight different levels of quality: Level '0' teachers did not do anything to clarify the learning goals for students, and Level '7' teachers read aloud the learning goals, gave examples, definitions, and/or connections to past or future activities, explained why the things students were about to learn were important, and engaged students in the process. The second study reduced the levels to six to qualify teachers' practices to clarify learning goals. In the second study, these researchers linked the quality of the teachers' practices to clarify learning goals with the students' understanding of them. Overall, the results of both studies indicated that very few teachers implemented practices at the highest level (only six of the 20 teachers in study 1, and two of the 58 in study 2). The practices most commonly observed in both studies corresponded to Level 2 and Level 3. An example of Level 2 practices is writing the learning goal on the board and reading it aloud. An example of Level 3 practices is defining words in the learning goal so that students can understand it clearly. Indeed, there is still much to learn about how to clarify learning goals effectively and engaging student in the process.

Criteria for Success

Success criteria, sometimes called "student look-fors" (Moss & Brookhart, 2012), are the characteristics of good work that students and teachers can use to examine formative assessment evidence to answer the questions "Where are we?" and "How will we get there?" Criteria for success make the learning goal clear to students. They can be shared with students in several ways, including "I can" statements, rubrics, checklists, guiding questions, or by analysis of sample student work (sometimes called "exemplars"). It is the criteria that provide the specific basis for student understanding of the learning target or goal, the specific reference points for feedback, and the yardstick by which progress toward the learning goal may be measured.

A common misconception is to confuse criteria with evidence or activities. For example, one of us once asked a teacher what criteria she would use to see whether students have learned. She replied, "I'll use their written paragraphs." The paragraphs are not criteria; they are the products that constitute the evidence of student learning to which criteria must be applied. In our example about finding the main idea, the criteria might include the following:

In my paragraph,

- I name a main idea that applies to the whole text.
- I show details from the text that support my main idea.

- I explain how the details are related to the main idea and why they support it.
- I use all the important details in the text.

In this lesson, both teacher feedback and student self-assessment should be focused on these criteria. To the extent that these criteria are met, the work is evidence of learning. To the extent that these criteria are not met, the work identifies areas for improvement.

When students understand the criteria for good work, the result is increased achievement, improved student self-assessment capabilities, and improved sense of control over one's learning. "Knowing where you're going" supports focused instruction and has motivational as well as learning benefits. For criteria to make learning goals clearer to the students, they need to address what students should look for in their work as evidence of achievement of the learning goals. For example, it is important for students to know what would count as quality or what evidence is required to know that they have learned. Only if we provide students with clear information in the criteria can they use it for feedback.

These claims have been demonstrated in many subject areas and grade levels: in primary-level projects (Higgins, Harris, & Kuehn, 1994); in elementary and middle school writing (Andrade, Du, & Wang, 2008; Andrade, Du, & Mycek, 2010; Coe, Hanita, Nishioka, & Smiley, 2011); in middle school mathematics (Ross, Hoagaboam-Gray, & Rolheiser, 2002) and special education (Lee & Lee, 2009); in secondary school social studies (Panadero, Tapia, & Huertas, 2012; Ross & Starling, 2008); and in college math (Yopp & Rehberger, 2009), biology (Hafner & Hafner, 2003), multimedia (Panadero, Alonso-Tapia, & Reche, 2013), and criminal justice (Howell, 2011). Table 2.1 succinctly describes some of these studies.

Finally, it is important to mention the results of a meta-analyses focusing on studies of quality of writing and feedback. Graham, Hebert, and Harris (2015) did a meta-analysis of studies of formative assessment in writing in grades one to eight. While they

Table 2.1 Empirical Evidence About the Importance of Learning Goals and Success Criteria

Authors	Gist of the Study	Explanation
Harris and Kuehn (Higgins, Harris, & Kuehn, 1994)	Young students can learn to help identify the qualities their work should have	Early in the school year, most of the criteria the students named were about group process (e.g., the group getting along together). In December, students viewed examples of projects, and with continued guidance and class discussion began to understand the importance of criteria centered on learning (e.g., the information contained in the project). By the end of the year, about half the criteria students chose were about process and half were about learning. This study shows that students need to *learn* how to focus on learning criteria and that they can start to do this as early as first grade.
Andrade, Du, and Wang (2008)	How exemplary products help to clarify, illustrate the learning goals, and improve feedback	Researchers asked third and fourth graders to read a model written assignment, produce their own list of criteria, and self-assess drafts of their writing, using rubrics. A comparison group of students brainstormed criteria and self-assessed their drafts, but did not use the rubric. Controlling for previous writing ability, the group that used the rubrics for self-assessment wrote better pieces overall, and specifically in the areas of ideas, organization, paragraphs, voice, and word choice. The quality of sentences and use of writing conventions did not differ between the groups; that is, the improvement in learning was found in the more substantive areas of writing. Andrade, Du, and Mycek

(Continued)

Table 2.1 (Continued)

Authors	Gist of the Study	Explanation
		(2010) replicated this study with middle school students in fifth, sixth, and seventh grade. The findings were similar, except that the rubric group's writing was evaluated as higher quality on all six criteria. When students are focused on specific criteria for success that define qualities of good writing, they give themselves better self-assessment feedback, and they write better.
Coe et al. (2011)	Test the effects of a rubric—a success criteria-based model—on quality of writing	This large-scale study tested the efficacy of the 6+1 Trait ® writing model (http://educationnorthwest.org/traits) that exemplifies success criteria using rubrics. The model is based on a rubric that describes characteristics (traits) of good writing to help teachers improve writing instruction and feedback, and to help both teachers and students better understand the qualities of good writing. The study included 196 teachers and more than 4,000 students in 74 schools. Researchers compared posttest essay scores of students whose teachers did and did not have professional development in using the 6+1 Trait ® writing model. Researchers controlled for students' previous writing performance, school and teacher characteristics, and accounted for the fact that students were grouped within schools. Students whos e teachers used the rubrics—the success criteria—improved significantly in three

Authors	Gist of the Study	Explanation
		of the six traits (Organization, Voice, and Word Choice). In the other three traits (Ideas, Sentence Fluency, and Conventions), students outperformed the control group but the difference did not reach statistical significance.
Ross, Hoagaboam-Gray, and Rolheiser (2002)	The importance of success criteria for self-assessment	Researchers gave fifth and sixth grade students self-assessment instruction in mathematics, based on success criteria. Their method used four strategies (p. 48): (1) involving students in defining criteria, (2) teaching them how to apply the criteria, (3) giving students feedback on these self-assessments against criteria, and (4) helping them develop action plans based on the self-assessments. Controlling for previous problem-solving ability, students who self-assessed using criteria outscored a comparison group at solving mathematics problems, with an effect size of 0.40.
Ross and Starling (2008)	The importance of criteria to focus on what students should look for in their work	Researchers used the same four-component self-assessment training as Ross, Hoagaboam-Gray, and Rolheiser (2002). Training focused on criteria, with secondary students in a ninth-grade geography class. These students were learning to solve geography problems using global information systems (GIS) software. Learning goals were about both accurate use of the software and about applying it to real-world geography problems, including being able to explain their problem solving strategies. Criteria addressed what students should look for in their work as evidence of their achievement of both of these learning goals.

(Continued)

Table 2.1 (Continued)

Authors	Gist of the Study	Explanation
		Controlling for pretest computer self-efficacy, the treatment group performed better than a comparison group on three different measures: production of a map using the software, a report explaining their problem-solving strategies, and an exam measuring knowledge of the mapping program. The largest difference was for the problem-solving explanations.
Panadero, Tapia, and Huertas (2012)	The importance of focusing students on their learning, either through learning goals or clear criteria, to improve learning and fostering self-regulation	Researchers designed a study with four independent variables: (1) type of instruction (oriented to process or to performance), (2) type of self-assessment tool (control vs. rubric vs. script), (3) feedback (oriented to process or to performance), and (4) task number (first through third; students did three tasks). The study compared students who used a rubric to assess their work (an assessment tool presenting a list of criteria with a set of performance level descriptions) with students who used a script (a series of self-reflection questions that walked students through the process of doing the task) and with a control group that used neither tool. The researchers hypothesized that rubrics would focus students more on the work product (the completed landscape analysis), and scripts would focus students more on the process of doing the task. This is the reason the other two independent variables about instruction—type of

Authors	*Gist of the Study*	*Explanation*
		instruction and type of feedback— also each had two groups focusing on process or product. Students who used rubrics or scripts outperformed the control group, suggesting either tool fostered learning. Although it is not possible to generalize from one study, it appears that the important thing is focusing students on their learning, not the particular format for the criteria. A focus on learning goals and criteria also fostered student self-regulation. Students who used scripts had the highest self-regulation scores, followed by those who used rubrics, and then the control group. The highest self-regulation was noted at the first task, decreasing over the second and third tasks.
Lee and Lee (2009)	Individualized Education Program (IEP) based on rubrics improved student engagement and performance	Researchers studied the effects of using instructional rubrics based on special education students' Individualized Education Program (IEP) goals on both class engagement and performance. They studied three fifth- and sixth-grade boys with mild intellectual disability, each in a class with 29 or 30 other students. The primary subjects, the three boys, had special rubrics based on their IEP goals, but all students in the three classes used rubrics based on learning goals (with three levels for the special students and four levels for the regular students). The classroom behaviors and engagement of the three boys improved, and the overall performance of students in all three classes improved significantly from pre-test to post-test.

judged the effect sizes from studies of the 6 + 1 Trait ® writing model as too small to be meaningful (effect sizes tell how big the difference is between a treatment group and a control group), they found effect sizes from the use of feedback in formative writing assessment in general to be significant and substantial. Feedback from adults had the largest effect on students' writing quality, with an average weighted effect size of 0.87, a large effect in education. Feedback from self-assessment (effect size of 0.62) and peer feedback (effect size of 0.58) had medium effect sizes, and even feedback from computers made a difference (effect size of 0.38).

Effective Feedback Is Based on Learning Goals and Success Criteria

The research reviewed in the previous section suggests that a good understanding of your learning goals and success criteria on the part of *students* leads to effective feedback: both effective self-assessment and the ability to effectively use teacher feedback. But the student is only half of the "learning team" in a classroom. Our formative assessment framework rests on the notion that learning is a social activity, and that it occurs in interactions that include both you and your students. We have seen many examples of teacher feedback to students that were inaccurate or even potentially might lead to students' development of misconceptions, when the *teacher* did not have a deep understanding of the learning goals herself.

Success criteria focus feedback on the aspects of evidence in students' work that are integral to the learning goal, and not surface features. Most of us remember receiving papers back from teachers on which the feedback was mostly copyediting rather than comments on the substance of the paper. Many teachers find it difficult to provide feedback that is likely to move students forward in their learning (Kroog, King Hess, & Ruiz-Primo, 2016; Ruiz-Primo & Li, 2004; Ruiz-Primo, Li, Ayala, & Shavelson, 2004; Schneider & Gowan, 2013). Similarly, many teachers find it difficult to decide on the next instructional moves (Heritage, Kim, Vendlinski, & Herman, 2009; Ruiz-Primo &

Kroog, 2017), which we consider as a type of feedback. When teachers *do* provide feedback that is likely to inform and motivate, and when they *do* select next instructional moves informed by students' current understanding, all parts of the formative assessment cycle—which is a learning cycle—benefit. Students get an even clearer understanding of the learning goal for which they are aiming, get information that is useful for improvement, and do in fact take next steps in learning.

One kind of simple feedback for students who just need a gentle nudge is "reminder feedback," where the teacher just restates for students what the learning target is (Clarke, 2003). If a student understands the learning target for a lesson, that may be all it takes to refocus a student's thoughts and actions on the goal. For students who need more help than that, Clarke describes "scaffolded feedback," for example, breaking down a task and asking small questions about each step. For students who are far from their learning target, Clarke suggests "example feedback," where the teacher models directly what the students' next steps might be.

In this chapter, based on extensive research, we are making the case that feedback should describe what students did well, according to the criteria for success on the learning goal they were demonstrating, and give at least one suggestion for improvement. These suggestions should also be based on the criteria for success. However, suggestions for improvement should not be a "laundry list" of everything that needs to be "fixed" in a work. That kind of feedback will overwhelm students and shut them down (Covington, 1992). To give effective feedback, you should make suggestions for a student's next steps in learning based on the learning goals and criteria, information from the student's work, plus pedagogical knowledge about common learning trajectories students take toward the goals and information about the student as a learner. Therefore, formative feedback requires that you learn something as well as the student, using the work as a window into student thinking.

Research into the formative assessment process is beginning to show that teachers who are expert at formative assessment use formative assessment evidence to understand student thinking

(Hattie, 2009; Kroog, Ruiz-Primo, & Sands, 2014; Minstrell, Anderson, & Li, 2009; Ruiz-Primo & Furtak, 2006, 2007; Ruiz-Primo, Iverson, & Sands, 2014). Understanding student thinking is necessary in order to provide feedback or immediate next instructional moves that will address specific needs. In contrast, teachers who are *not* expert at formative assessment collect evidence of the level or amount of student performance, usually in the form of correctness of responses, and re-teach topics where scores were low. This re-teaching may or may not address misunderstandings; after all, the first round of teaching did not, and nothing has changed.

Understanding Learning Goals

We have tried to make the point that effective feedback is based on learning goals and criteria for success. Before sharing learning targets and defining success criteria there is an important requisite: clarity of the learning goals being pursued and why they are important for students to achieve. Although this idea may look simple to you, it is not. Deep understanding of the learning goals of a unit does not occur spontaneously. It extends far beyond a listing of the learning objectives that typically appear at the beginning of a unit, module, or chapter (Ruiz-Primo & Li, 2009; Ruiz-Primo et al., 2012; Ruiz-Primo, 2016).

Deep understanding of the learning goals requires being able to respond to questions such as: What is to be learned? Why am I teaching this content? Why is this learning important for my students in the context of the unit/module/topic or chapter, and even beyond? How are these learning goals to be achieved—that is, what instructional activities and tasks will help my students make progress in their learning? Why are the activities in this unit sequenced in the way that they are? How does each activity contribute to achievement of the overall learning targets and goals? What critical foundational blocks of knowledge, practices, or skills need to be established to achieve the learning goals? What specific evidence will show that those foundational elements have been built? How will I know that students have learned what I intend? What evidence do I need to demonstrate that the learning goals have been met? These questions, together, constitute an effective framework for thinking about feedback episodes (Ruiz-Primo, 2016). In our experience, when we have asked teachers why they are teaching what they are teaching, the response is never straightforward. Furthermore, it is hard for teachers to explain the progression that a unit follows to develop deeper and more sophisticated students' understanding in any given topic.

Developing a Deeper Understanding of Learning Goals

How can you develop a deeper understanding of the unit that can lead to a better understanding of the learning goals and the definition of success criteria? Ruiz-Primo and Li (2009) proposed a process named *mapping* to develop a better understanding of a unit to be taught. The purpose of mapping is twofold: (a) to *understand the learning goal(s)* to be met at the end of a unit, and (b) to *understand how these learning goals are to be achieved* by the teacher and students. Mapping is an iterative process that allows teachers to discern the essence of a unit by moving back and forth between two levels of analysis: the lesson and the unit as a whole. It helps teachers to grasp at a deeper level the essence of the *intended curriculum* by identifying the concepts, processes, problem-solving approaches, proof schemes, or principles that are critical in each lesson of the unit and understanding how they become interrelated from one lesson to the next.

These researchers implemented this process in an assessment project related to science (Ruiz-Primo & Li, 2008). They asked teachers, working in groups of three or four, to identify the learning pursued in each lesson, along with the instructional activities proposed in the unit to achieve those learning goals. They provided teachers with a tool, *unit maps*, that track seven aspects of each lesson within a unit or module (see Figure 2.1): (a) the learning goals for the lesson; in their project they focused on the scientific knowledge and scientific processes; (b) the type of knowledge in which students would be engaged (in their case they focused on declarative, procedural, and schematic knowledge);

| Lesson | Learning Targets | | | Type of Knowledge Involved | | | Activities supporting the achievement of targets ... |
	Disciplinary core idea	Science & engineering practices	Crosscutting concept	Declarative knowledge	Procedural knowledge	Schematic knowledge	
1							
2							
3							
...							
n							

Figure 2.1 Module map template for science modules (Adapted from Ruiz-Primo & Li, 2009).

(c) the activities that are critical to achieve the learning goals for the lesson; (d) the documentation required from students; (e) the materials used; (f) the graphical representations that students would deal with; and (g) the vocabulary involved in the lesson. Some of these aspects were critical for the project in which this process was immersed.

They asked teachers to go back and forth among the lessons to review and make any necessary changes to the learning goals and the criticality of the activities. As teachers analyzed the lessons it became clear what was critical and what was not for future lessons: what seemed important in an initial analysis may have appeared less or unimportant once subsequent lessons were analyzed, or vice versa, something that initially seemed unimportant became important in a future lesson. "The more fully the teacher understands a lesson and how it contributes to achieving the unit learning goal, the more closely in tune will be the learning targets and critical activities across lessons" (Ruiz-Primo, 2016, p. 225). We found that teachers indicated that the mapping experience impacted their understanding of the units. For instance, one teacher stated:

We learned a lot from mapping the curriculum, and from each other. The ability to talk about what activities really help us get the kids to the learning goal. Nobody helps us filter out what is not important . . . and the opposite; sometimes we have filtered out the most important pieces/ activities cuz [sic] *we didn't really understand their purpose.*

Teachers' mapping discussions also provided evidence to evaluate the characteristics of the mapping approach. For example, teachers agreed that

Thinking about those types of knowledge [declarative, procedural, and schematic knowledge] *really led us through the process. It was very helpful for this structure* [pointing to the unit map]. *When we looked at the learning progression, we could see where the learning targets could move from declarative to schematic with the right experiences and scaffolding.*

After teachers mapped the learning targets and other critical information for each lesson in a unit, they then made informed decisions about the overarching unit learning goal(s). In addition, mapping a unit helped them understand how well students were being supported to develop successively more sophisticated thinking about the topic at hand.

Defining the trajectory that students will follow in a unit can help to (a) clarify critical concepts that are prerequisite to others, (b) define how critical concepts are connected, and (c) pinpoint students' knowledge and performance at any given point of time (on the trajectory) in the unit. Understanding the unit helps you to know how to better engage students in the learning and assessment process. It not only helps you to clarify the learning goals, but also to define what criteria should be used to assess whether they were achieved.

Embodying Learning Goals and Criteria in Tasks and Rubrics

If we have succeeded in convincing you that effective feedback is based on learning goals and criteria for success, then the obvious next step is to make sure that the tasks your students are asked to do elicit evidence of learning—not just following directions—and the rubrics or other assessment tools used to evaluate performance describe student thinking and learning—again, not following directions. In this book, we do not describe all the steps in creating effective tasks and rubrics, but limit our discussion to assuring that effective tasks embody learning goals and that effective rubrics examine student performance on the tasks using criteria that describe learning. Effective feedback can only happen when this is the case.

A task embodies learning goals for students if doing the task will show how well they have learned. This is the case whether the "task" is answering a test question, participating in a class discussion, creating a model of something, writing an essay, solving a problem, or giving a report.

For example, a common language arts standard asks students to identify the main idea in a text and support this main idea with details from the text. To elicit evidence of whether students can do that, a task would need to present students with text.

The text would have to be at the appropriate reading level and it would have to be about a topic on which the student had sufficient background knowledge. This much might seem obvious. A less obvious, but equally important, consideration is that the text should be something the students had not already interpreted together in class. For example, if students had already discussed Martin Luther King, Jr.'s "I Have a Dream" speech in class, then a task which asked them to identify the main idea in the speech and support it with details in the speech would *not* be an indicator of student achievement of the learning goal. It would, rather, be an indicator of students' ability to recall what was said in class, perhaps an important skill but not the skill about which the teacher needs evidence.

Another common example of a mismatch between a learning goal and a task is what are sometimes called "retelling" tasks (Dodge, 2002). Retelling tasks ask students to retrieve some information and reproduce it. Examples include:

- Make a poster about a planet and list six facts about the planet.
- Write a report about a country of your choice.
- Make a slide presentation about one grouping of elements in the periodic table and present it to the class.

We have seen hundreds of such tasks; they abound in classrooms at all levels. In retelling tasks, information can simply be transferred from print or electronic sources to the desired format (e.g., poster, report, slide presentation). Retelling tasks give evidence that students retrieved the right information, not that they have memorized it, or understand it, or have in any sense "learned" it. Most learning goals do not ask students to retrieve information. At the least, they ask students to comprehend information.

More effective learning goals ask students to do something with information, for example, solve a problem or make a connection between the information and another text or scenario or one's own life. It is important that the task match the learning goal not only by topic, but also by cognitive level. For example, if students are supposed to be able to analyze poems, learning and assessment tasks should ask them to do that and not, for example, recite a poem or write an original poem. If a task does not embody the learning goal, it will not give evidence that can be interpreted to show students' progress toward that learning goal.

Similarly, with the wrong criteria, feedback is misdirected. It is not enough to have a task match a learning goal; the criteria by which performance is assessed must match, as well. To continue our poem example, if a learning goal asks students to interpret imagery in poems, they might be given a poem to read with directions to write a paragraph describing how the imagery in the poem contributes to its meaning. If feedback about students' paragraphs comes mostly in the form of correcting grammar and usage, the evidence of student thinking about imagery contained in the paragraphs will be wasted.

It is unfortunately very common to see rubrics where the criteria are more about following directions than about evidence of thinking and learning. For example, we have seen rubrics for reports where what is assessed is whether the reports have "required elements" (e.g., a title, name and date, and so on, as well as parts of the report), have "three pictures," use good grammar, and the like. The problem with such rubrics is that student work is not assessed for evidence of understanding of the learning goal, but rather for evidence of following directions. As a result, students can mistakenly think they are understanding well when they are not. This can lead to surprises when, for example, high school students who thought they were very good at science—because they "gave the teacher everything she wanted"—get to college and take a science course and find they really don't understand the subject very well!

Here is one compelling example: Students in a seventh-grade science class were assigned to write "biome reports" and present them to the class. If the teacher's goal had been to have students understand that biomes are large-scale communities of organisms affected by common patterns of climate and geology, then the assignment didn't match. The biome report was a retelling activity. Students had to reproduce a map of where the biome is located, list facts about its climate, vegetation, and wildlife, and include pictures. Most students put their maps and pictures into their reports by copying images from the Internet.

Even worse, the criteria did not match the intended learning outcomes, with very sad results for one student. There were nine criteria on the rubric for the biome report, based on which students received feedback and, ultimately, a grade. The nine criteria were Required content (title page elements); World map locating the biome; Facts (at least five); Climate (separate paragraph); Pictures of animals (at least five); Pictures of plants (at least three); Grammar; Attractiveness and organization; and Professionalism of presentation. A quick glance at this list is all that is required to see that these "criteria" were not about the learning goal, but about following the directions for the assignment (there were also too many criteria).

One of the students in this class received a good evaluation with this feedback: "Only counted three facts in your opening paragraph" and "Excellent work during your presentation." His report was about Temperate Forests. He had reproduced the requisite number of pictures from electronic sources. His paragraphs, while including most of the required facts, were very brief. Another student did not reproduce pictures, but his paragraphs were longer and much more detailed than the first student. Evidence from the actual content of his writing suggested the second student understood more about Temperate Grasslands than the first student had understood about Temperate Forests. But his evaluation was dismal—in fact, he failed the assignment. He received this feedback: "Lacking period number [on the title page]"; "Map should be enlarged"; and, next to the criteria about pictures of animals and plants, "Why [no pictures]?" The teacher's final comment was, "The rubric was not followed to complete assignment. Project lacked pictures and a detailed map."

This story is a true one, and it breaks our hearts. A student who arguably understood more about the learning goal was misassessed as a failure, and a student who perhaps did not understand as much was assessed as a great success, not because of their work or their evidence of learning, but because the assessment and especially the criteria did not match the intended learning goal. Teachers with whom we have shared this story have dubbed the offending criteria "killer rubrics."

It is not that the requirements for the assignment are unimportant. A checklist can be useful for keeping track of requirements, either for self- or peer assessment, or for checking to see whether an assignment is ready to be turned in. We are not arguing that you should accept incomplete work or that following directions is not an important skill. We are arguing that criteria for assessing student work should be about the substance of the learning goal; that is, they should examine student thinking. If the biome assignment had been a better one and not simply a retelling, one of the criteria, for example, might have been about the quality of students' explanations of how climate affected the vegetation in the biome. We are also arguing that the performance-level descriptions for each of the criteria—those descriptions of what work looks like at all levels of performance—should be about the quality of the work and not simple counts (e.g., "explanation is detailed and reasons are given," not "contains 5 facts"). The latter result is a test-score-style assessment disguised as rubrics and is not useful for formative assessment and feedback (Minstrell, Anderson, & Li, 2009).

Closing Comments

Feedback, like everything else in the formative learning cycle, is based on learning goals and criteria for success. Learning goals come at different grain sizes, and are instantiated in classrooms by all sorts of different tasks. Even at the level of a learning target for an individual lesson, however, students should know what it is they are supposed to be learning and the criteria by which their learning will be assessed. Research suggests that students who are clear on criteria produce better work and are more self-regulated learners. Research suggests that teachers who are clear on criteria use student work as evidence of student learning, and use their insights to provide feedback and select next instructional moves. Research also suggests that this wonderful state of affairs is not yet typical, and that it is difficult for teachers, at least as currently trained and supported, to accomplish.

However, there is enough evidence that it can be done. The chapter has provided some practical suggestions about how to make tasks and rubrics (or other criteria) embody and give evidence of the goals of learning. In the next chapter, we turn to characteristics of effective feedback. How does one select comments and instructional moves that feed a student forward from his current place in the formative learning cycle and help him move closer to the learning goal?

References

Andrade, H. L., Du, Y., & Mycek, K. (2010). Rubric-referenced self-assessment and middle school students' writing. *Assessment in Education, 17*(2), 199–214.

Andrade, H. L., Du, Y., & Wang, X. (2008). Putting rubrics to the test: The effect of a model, criteria generation, and rubric-referenced self-assessment on elementary students' writing. *Educational Measurement: Issues and Practice, 27*(2), 3–13.

Bransford, J. D., Brown, A. L., & Cocking, R. R. (2000). *How people learn: Brain, mind, experience, and school* (Expanded ed.). Washington, DC: National Academy Press.

Brown, A. L., Kane, M. J., & Echols, C. H. (1986). Young children's mental models determine analogical transfer across problems with common goal structure. *Cognitive Development, 1*, 103–121.

Clarke, S. (2003). *Enriching feedback in the primary classroom.* London: Hodder Murray.

Coe, M., Hanita, M., Nishioka, V., & Smiley, R. (2011, December). *An investigation of the impact of the 6+1 Trait Writing Model on grade 5 student writing achievement: Final report* (NCEE Report 2012–4010). Washington, DC: U.S. Department of Education.

Covington, M. V. (1992). *Making the grade: A self-worth perspective on motivation and school reform.* Cambridge: Cambridge University Press.

Dodge, B. (2002). *WebQuest taskonomy: A taxonomy of tasks.* Retrieved from http://webquest.org/sdsu/taskonomy.html

Eraut, M. (1997). Perspectives on defining 'The Learning Society'. *Journal of Education Policy, 12*(6), 551–558.

Graham, S., Hebert, M., & Harris, K. R. (2015). Formative assessment and writing: A meta-analysis. *The Elementary School Journal, 115*, 523–547.

Hafner, J. C., & Hafner, P. M. (2003). Quantitative analysis of the rubric as an assessment tool: An empirical study of student peer-group rating. *International Journal of Science Education, 25*(12), 1509–1528.

Hattie, J. A. C. (2009). *Visible learning: A synthesis of over 800 meta-analyses relating to achievement*. London: Routledge.

Hattie, J. A. C., & Timperley, H. (2007). The power of feedback. *Review of Educational Research, 77*(1), 81–112.

Heritage, M. (2010). *Formative assessment: Making it happen in the classroom*. Thousand Oaks, CA: Corwin.

Heritage, M., Kim, J., Vendlinski, T., & Herman, J. (2009). From evidence to action: A seamless process in formative assessment? *Educational Measurement: Issues and Practice, 28*(3), 24–31.

Higgins, K. M., Harris, N. A., & Kuehn, L. L. (1994). Placing assessment into the hands of young children: A study of student-generated criteria and self-assessment. *Educational Assessment, 2*(4), 309–324.

Howell, R. J. (2011). Exploring the impact of grading rubrics on academic performance : findings from a quasi-experimental, pre-post evaluation. *Journal on Excellence in College Teaching, 22*(2), 31–49.

Kroog, H. I., King Hess, K., & Ruiz-Primo, M. A. (2016). Implement effective and efficient approaches to formal formative assessment that will save time and boost student learning. *Educational Leadership, 73*(7), 22–25.

Kroog, H. I., & Ruiz-Primo, M. A. (2015). The practices used by teachers to clarify and share learning goals and the alignment between student's and teacher's perceptions of these goals. Paper under review.

Kroog, H. I., Ruiz-Primo, M. A., & Sands, D. (2014). *Understanding the interplay between the cultural context of classrooms and formative assessment*. Paper presented at the annual meeting of the American Educational Research Association, Philadelphia, PA.

Lee, E., & Lee, S. (2009). Effects of instructional rubrics on class engagement behaviors and the achievement of lesson objectives by students with mild mental retardation and their typical peers. *Education and Training in Developmental Disabilities, 44*(3), 396–408.

Minstrell, J., Anderson, R., & Li, M. (2009). *Assessing teacher competency in formative assessment*. Annual Report to the National Science Foundation. Alexandria, VA: National Science Foundation.

Moss, C. M., & Brookhart, S. M. (2012). *Learning targets: Helping students aim for understanding in today's lesson*. Alexandria, VA: ASCD.

Moss, C. M., Brookhart, S. M., & Long, B. A. (2013). Administrators' roles in helping teachers use formative assessment information. *Applied Measurement in Education, 26*, 205–218.

Panadero, E., Alonso-Tapia, J., & Reche, E. (2013). Rubrics vs. self-assessment scripts: Effect on self-regulation, performance and self-efficacy in pre-service teachers. *Studies in Educational Evaluation*, *39*, 125–132.

Panadero, E., Tapia, J. A., & Huertas, J. A. (2012). Rubrics and self-assessment scripts effects on self-regulation, learning and self-efficacy in secondary education. *Learning and Individual Differences*, *22*(6), 806–813. doi:10.1016/j.lindif.2012.04.007

Ross, J. A., Hoagaboam-Gray, A., & Rolheiser, C. (2002). Student self-evaluation in grade 5–6 mathematics: Effects on problem-solving achievement. *Educational Assessment*, *8*, 43–58.

Ross, J. A., & Starling, M. (2008). Self-assessment in a technology-supported environment: The case of grade 9 geography. *Assessment in Education*, *15*(2), 183–199.

Ruiz-Primo, M. A. (2016). Implementing high quality assessment for learning: Mapping as a professional development tool for understanding the *what to learn*, *why to learn it*, and *how to learn it*. In D. Laveault & L. Allal (Eds.). *Assessment for learning—meeting the challenge of implementation* (pp. 219–236). Switzerland: Springer International Publishing.

Ruiz-Primo, M. A., & Furtak, E. M. (2006). Informal formative assessment and scientific inquiry: Exploring teachers' practices and student learning. *Educational Assessment*, *11*(3–4), 205–235.

Ruiz-Primo, M. A., & Furtak, E. M. (2007). Exploring teachers' informal formative assessment practices and students' understanding in the context of scientific inquiry. *Journal of Research in Science Teaching*, *44*(1), 57–84.

Ruiz-Primo, M. A., Iverson, H., & Sands, D. (2014, April). *Looking at feedback practices in science and mathematics classrooms: Lessons learned*. Symposium: Examining Feedback Practices in Multiple Settings with Multiple perspectives. Paper presented at the American Educational Research Association Annual Meeting, Philadelphia, PA.

Ruiz-Primo, M. A., & Kroog, H. (2015). *The impact of observation sampling strategies on the accuracy of inferences about teachers' formative assessment practices*. Paper submitted for publication. Paper under review.

Ruiz-Primo, M. A., & Kroog, H. (2017, April). *Variations of formative assessment practices across instructional tasks*. Paper presented at the AERA annual meeting, San Antonio, TX.

Ruiz-Primo, M. A., & Li, M. (2004). On the use of students' science notebooks as an assessment tool. *Studies in Educational Evaluation*, *30*, 61–85.

Ruiz-Primo, M. A., & Li, M. (2008). *Building a methodology for developing and evaluating instructionally sensitive assessments*. Proposal submitted and awarded to the National Science Foundation. Award ID: DRL-0816123.

Ruiz-Primo, M. A., & Li, M. (2009). *Mapping the intended curriculum*. Internal document. Developing and evaluating instructionally sensitive assessments (DEISA) project. University of Colorado Denver: School of Education and Human Development, Laboratory of Educational Assessment, Research and InnovatioN (LEARN).

Ruiz-Primo, M. A., Li, M., Ayala, C. C., & Shavelson, R. J. (2004). Evaluating students' science notebooks as an assessment tool. *International Journal of Science Education*, 26(12), 1477–1506.

Ryan, R. M., & Deci, E. L. (2000). Intrinsic and extrinsic motivations: Classic definitions and new directions. *Contemporary Educational Psychology*, 25, 54–67.

Ruiz-Primo, M. A., Li., M., Wills, K., Giamellaro, M., Lan, M-C., Mason, H., Sands, D. (2012). Developing and evaluating instructionally sensitive assessments in science. *Journal of Research in Science Teaching, 49*(6), 691–712.

Sadler, D. R. (1989). Formative assessment and the design of instructional systems. *Instructional Science, 18*, 119–144.

Schneider, M. C., & Gowan, P. (2013). Investigating teachers' skills in interpreting evidence of student learning. *Applied Measurement in Education, 26*, 191–204. doi:10.1080/08957347.2013.793185

Sztajn, P., Confrey, J., Wilson, P. H., & Edgington, C. (2012). Learning trajectory based instruction: Toward a theory of teaching. *Educational Researcher, 41*(5), 147–156. doi:10.3102/0013189X12442801

Wiliam, D. (2010). An integrative summary of the research literature and implications for a new theory of formative assessment. In H. L. Andrade & G. J. Cizek (Eds.), *Handbook of formative assessment* (pp. 18–40). New York: Routledge.

Wiliam, D. (2016). *Leadership for teacher learning: Creating a culture where all teachers improve so that all learners succeed*. West Palm Beach, FL: Learning Sciences International.

Yopp, D., & Rehberger, R. (2009). A curriculum focus intervention's effects on prealgebra achievement. *Journal of Developmental Education, 33*(2), 28–30.

3

Characteristics of
Effective Feedback
Comments and Instructional Moves

Chapter 1 gave you a framework for considering classroom formative assessment, of which feedback is a key component. Chapter 2 showed how feedback needs to be derived from and related to the goals for learning in order for feedback to function formatively—to help students move toward those learning goals. This chapter examines characteristics of effective feedback, considering both comments and instructional moves as types of feedback. Both are responses to the formative assessment evidence found in students' work, or in observation of the processes students used to do their work. Both require inferences about what the work product or process says about the students' status in relationship to learning goals.

We begin with the idea to make feedback an episode of learning not only for students, but also for the teacher. Next we focus on feedback as an episode of learning for students. This section describes characteristics of effective comments and instructional moves. We end the chapter by proposing a guide to think about feedback as comments or instructional moves. The persistent findings in the feedback literature that not all feedback is helpful points to the fact that something more is going on than simply crafting and delivering appropriate comments. Recent developments in formative assessment research and in research on the self-regulation and co-regulation of learning give us a clue to that missing component. We discuss some of these issues in the last section of the chapter.

Feedback as an Episode of Learning for the Teacher

The role of teacher feedback to students in a well-functioning formative assessment cycle is to help students move from their current state of understanding to the next step in the development of mastery of a learning goal. This can only be accomplished effectively and efficiently by teachers who learn what students are thinking. Teachers who merely "correct students' work" miss the key opportunity to target their comments—or their next instructional moves (see next section)—to students' learning needs. While these conclusions stem from research into teachers' formative assessment practices, a similar conclusion results when synthesizing feedback research broadly—what some might call the "30,000 foot" view.

In his book *Visible Learning*, Hattie (2009) reported that prior to his major synthesis of meta-analyses, he had already synthesized many reviews of feedback and famously prescribed that students should receive "dollops" (p. 173) of feedback. However, his thinking about feedback changed as he reviewed more of the research evidence. He began to think of feedback as something beyond the responses teachers provide to students about their work. He wrote (p. 173):

> It was only when I discovered that feedback was most powerful when it is from the *student to the teacher* [italics in original] that I started to understand it better. When teachers seek, or at least are open to, feedback from students as to what students know, what they understand, where they make errors, when they have misconceptions, when they are not engaged—then teaching and learning can be synchronized and powerful.

In other words, feedback should be an episode of learning for both student *and* teacher, and the teacher should concentrate on using a feedback episode to learn about student thinking and understanding. The role of teacher feedback to students in the formative assessment cycle is to move students' thinking from the level demonstrated in the work to the next step in the development of mastery of a learning goal.

Teachers who use formative assessment effectively collect evidence of how students are understanding concepts, processes, problem-solving approaches, or principles and where they have misconceptions. They get this information from students' work on assignments and from what students say. Then, they consider what comments or immediate next step in instruction will take the student from that point to the next logical step in learning. This maximizes the effect of feedback on student learning.

In contrast, teachers who are *not* effective with formative assessment limit their collection of evidence to the correctness of student work. Then, they make corrections or give assignments to review areas where students didn't "get a lot right." This is not a very effective approach. Such a teacher might, for example, assign a student another problem set of "two-digit addition" because the student didn't do very well with the first set, without addressing what specifically the student needed to learn (was carrying the problem? place value? basic facts?). The student may waste valuable learning time re-presenting to the teacher the same evidence of understanding, without making much progress.

This difference is illustrated in a study of professional development in formative assessment with science teachers that videotaped teachers using the formative assessment process (Minstrell, Anderson, & Li, 2009). They found that while different teachers may appear to be doing the same formative assessment process—gathering data, interpreting it, and acting on the findings—there was a big difference in the quality of their formative assessment. They distinguished two groups of teachers. The more expert teachers used a learner or learning-driven stance, determining how students were learning and moving forward from there. These teachers asked what students were thinking in relation to learning goals, interpreted the implications of this thinking for students' learning, and then designed feedback or instructional moves accordingly. The less expert teachers used curriculum-based assessment to determine how much students learned (percent correct) and what to re-teach. These teachers asked, "How many of my students have 'got it'?" For students who did not "get" whatever was being taught, teachers assigned review work.

Like Minstrell and his colleagues, in the DEMFAP project, Ruiz-Primo and her colleagues categorized teachers' lessons from high to low implementation and effectiveness of formative assessment practices, and then viewed how their videotaped lessons differed. They found that teachers who are expert in formative assessment spend the first day of a class helping students understand what learning goals are and why they are important, encouraging students to ask questions, and teaching students that they are responsible for their own learning. Teachers who are beginners at formative assessment focus their first day of class mainly on procedural issues such as grading, attendance, and tardy policies (Kroog, Ruiz-Primo, & Sands, 2014).

Before deciding what comments or instructional moves are needed, teachers need to look for feedback from students as to what they know and understand, what types of error they make, what misconceptions they have, and how to improve their engagement in learning.

Feedback as an Episode of Learning for the Student

Feedback becomes *formative* if it has the potential to influence student learning; if it helps students to reach higher levels of understanding relative to where they were before the information was collected (Sadler, 1989; Hargreaves, McCallum, & Gipps, 2000). For feedback (whether a comment or an instructional move) to have a meaningful effect on a given student's strategies and learning, the student *needs to understand it and use it.* Feedback is only effective and relevant if a student appropriately modifies her thinking process. Formative feedback should improve students' repertoires by pointing to strategies that can help them to reason and monitor themselves in order to perceive when their performance is falling short. Feedback needs to lead students to reflect on what they did, indicate what they need to do next, describe why something is right or wrong, or describe what they have attained and what they have not. It should help students to pay attention to errors or mistakes in a way that benefits their learning and stimulates thinking and ideas (Boaler, 2016). Each time a student makes a mistake, there is a potential for the student to grow, but *only if* the feedback helps the student see connections that were not previously identified. What led to the mistake? What connections did students make that led them to approach the problem in a different manner than expected? What task characteristics allow for growth and improvement?

In other words, to put it rather bluntly, feedback is useless if it is not readily intelligible to the student, if it does not help her to understand, remember, improve her knowledge, develop her skills, or extend her learning strategies (Perrenoud, 1998). We have seen many written comments on students' products and heard many oral comments made during class. Strictly speaking, however, these cannot be considered feedback because the comments or the instructional moves do not allow or invite the students to do something with the information provided or because the students cannot even understand them (Ruiz-Primo & Li, 2004, 2013).

In what follows we provide some characteristics of feedback, based on research, that may help you to make some decisions to craft more effective feedback. The characteristics presented are probabilistic in nature, that is, they are associated with increased student achievement *on average*. However, it is important to keep in mind there is still variation from student to student. Also, it is important to consider that the research cited focuses more on feedback as comments than feedback as instructional moves. Still, the characteristics are applicable to both comments and instructional moves.

Comments as Feedback: Characteristics of Effective Feedback Messages

Reviews of the feedback literature in general (Bangert-Drowns, Kulik, Kulik, & Morgan, 1991; Butler & Winne, 1995; Hattie &

Timperley, 2007; Kluger & DeNisi, 1996; Shute, 2008) and with an eye toward informing computer-based feedback (Mason & Bruning, 2001; Mory, 2004; Van der Kleij, Feskens, & Eggen, 2015) have converged on several characteristics for crafting and delivering effective feedback (Shute, 2008). Other researchers have studied the characteristics of crafting effective feedback comments directly, focusing specifically on the wording of comments (Johnston, 2004; Tunstall & Gipps, 1996). We present these characteristics by describing the kinds of decisions you have to make when deciding what to say (for oral feedback) or write (for written feedback), or do (for instructional moves). These characteristics have been presented elsewhere, as well (Brookhart, 2017). We organize the characteristics in a set of three practitioner-friendly categories: *context* in which the feedback is provided, *target* of the feedback, *attributes* of the feedback.

Context in Which the Feedback Is Provided

TIMING AND TASK CHARACTERISTICS

You have choices about when to give feedback: immediately or after some delay. Most research has found that feedback that occurs close in time to when student work is done is the most effective (Crooks, 1988; Hattie & Timperley, 2007; Kluger & DeNisi, 1996; Shute, 2008). Immediate feedback is warranted for knowledge of facts, where an answer is "right" or "wrong." Think of the answers listed on the back of math facts flashcards. However, for more complex tasks, especially for tasks requiring higher-order thinking, and for high-achieving students, consider using slightly delayed feedback so that students have time to do some processing of their own (Shute, 2008).

AUDIENCE AND INSTRUCTIONAL MODE

You must decide whether to give feedback to individual students, a small group of students, or the whole class. Most of the feedback research presumes individual feedback. Indeed, individual feedback, when it is possible, is usually best to meet the student needs. Benjamin Bloom, a noted educational researcher who spent much of his career on a research agenda he characterized as "the search for methods of group instruction as effective as one-to-one tutoring" (Bloom, 1984, p. 4), noted that formative assessment with what he called "individual correctives"—which we would now call feedback—can be carried out in classroom groups but can approach the level of effectiveness of individual tutoring. Individual feedback is one of the mechanisms by which this happens. However, sometimes in classes, a small group of students or the whole class may need very similar feedback, and feedback is given to those audiences. Feedback to small or whole-class groups amounts to using instructional moves as feedback.

MODE

Feedback can be delivered orally or in writing, or by demonstration—and of course, sometimes by computer. For students who are able to read, written feedback is generally recommended for major feedback episodes (Shute, 2008). For all students, individual oral feedback during work time is a staple of classroom practice. The key is to focus those brief episodes of oral feedback on criteria, positioning them as part of the formative assessment cycle and not simply chat. For some physical skills (e.g., how to hold a pencil), demonstrations can be part of feedback. Demonstration can also be given for more academic skills, for instance, how to revise a paragraph one has written, taking advantage of the fact that students learn much from observation and modeling (Ormrod, 2014). Feedback varies from one context to the next in the form in which it is provided and in the information it conveys. Writing comments is a more natural act in an assignment, homework, or quiz; oral comments in the context of dialogic interactions; and instructional moves and comments during whole classroom discussion.

Content of the Feedback

FOCUS

Feedback can focus on the work itself, the process the student used to do the work, or the process of student self-regulation; it should not focus on the student personally (Hattie & Timperley, 2007). Hattie and Timperley (2007) distinguished these four categories of feedback and described how the first three of them fit with the formative learning cycle. Feedback that focuses on the learning task is generally most effective (Crooks, 1988; Koenka, Moshontz, Atkinson, Sanchez, & Cooper, 2016). Feedback that focuses on the student personally (e.g., "You're so smart!") has a detrimental effect in that it helps students create the conception that intelligence is fixed and that learning is not under students' control. This fixed mindset leads to students being concerned with looking smart, avoiding challenges, and coping poorly with setbacks (Dweck, 2000).

AGENCY EMPHASIS

The words used in feedback should position students as the agents of their own learning. The manner in which teachers talk with students sets up their expectations (Johnston, 2004). Asking a student "What were you thinking as a writer?" implies that the student is a writer, not merely someone who carries out the teacher's instructions. This makes a big difference in how students will perceive and be able to use feedback. Covington (1992) would call this part of "motivational equity." He pointed out that students may have differing cognitive abilities, educational backgrounds, and interests, but all students should have access to feedback and instruction that enhances their belief that their effort on appropriate tasks will lead them to achieve appropriate learning goals.

REFERENCE OR COMPARISON FOR
INTERPRETING QUALITY

There are three basic ways to assess the quality of student work. *Normative or norm-referenced* feedback compares a student's work to the work of other students (e.g., Jack is better at writing descriptive paragraphs than Jill). *Criterion-referenced* feedback compares a student's work to a set of standards or criteria for good work (e.g., Jack's descriptive paragraph uses descriptive adjectives, vivid verbs, and strong images that appeal to the senses). This kind of feedback is (or should be!) used with a standards-based approach to instruction and assessment. *Self-referenced* feedback compares a student's work to expectations for that student, based on past performance (e.g., the descriptive paragraph Jack wrote today is much better than the one he wrote yesterday).

Criterion-referenced or standards-based feedback, based on what we have been calling success criteria or criteria for good work in the formative assessment framework, is best for most classroom purposes (Bangert-Drowns et al., 1991; Brookhart, 2017; Hattie & Timperley, 2007). Bangert-Drowns and colleagues found that, among 58 effect sizes from 40 studies, the mean effect was 0.26, and 18 of the effects were negative. However, if they selected effect sizes just from studies with no pre-test, no pre-search availability (students could not look up answers), with corrective (criterion-referenced) feedback on text comprehension tasks or classroom tests, the mean effect on learning was 0.77, a much larger effect. The type of comparison makes a big difference. In addition, a classroom atmosphere characterized by norm-referenced feedback supports the fixed mindset described above. Norm-referencing focuses students on outperforming their peers, not on learning (Stiggins & Conklin, 1992).

Attributes of the Feedback

FUNCTION

You should give descriptive, not evaluative, feedback, whenever possible. Evaluative feedback—whether in the form of a grade or in the form of evaluative comments like "Outstanding" (without describing what makes the work outstanding)—are not as conducive to learning (Koenka et al., 2016; Reeve, 2002) and are not preferred by students (Gamlem & Smith, 2013). The key is that students need to experience the feedback as descriptive, not evaluative. Deci and Ryan (1985) call this the *functional signifi-cance* of feedback. Feedback that is meant to be descriptive, but is written in a judgmental tone, may be experienced as evaluative. Feedback should draw students' attention to the task, describing strengths of the work and giving suggestions for next steps (commonly called "constructive criticism"). When such feedback includes support for these next steps and conveys the idea that the student is the agent of this learning, it can be called "constructing the way forward" (Tunstall & Gipps, 1996, p. 394).

VALENCE

"Valence" is used here as a metaphor to mean positive or negative. It is best for your feedback to begin by describing the strengths of students' work against the criteria for success with the learning goal. Often teachers assume that if students did something well, they know what they did and why they did it. That is a dangerous assumption to make, as it is often not true. Instead, "name and notice" (Johnston, 2004, p. 11) what students do well, helping them articulate where they are in their journey to the learning goal. Positive feedback includes such descriptions of strength and also suggestions for improvement that are made in such a way as to support students' next steps (Tunstall & Gipps, 1996). Students appreciate this kind of feedback (Gamlem & Smith, 2013).

Negative feedback, on the other hand, includes evaluative judgments about weaknesses of the work without description or without any suggestions for improvement that a student could reasonably take (Tunstall & Gipps, 1996). Some students experience this kind of feedback as disapproval and report that it makes them feel "useless" (Gamlem & Smith, 2013, p. 160).

CLARITY

Feedback needs to be clear to the student. Your students will not use feedback if they do not understand it, and they need to understand feedback before they will have the confidence to use it to revise their work or focus their studying. Feedback should use vocabulary that students understand, and the content of feedback should be tailored to students' developmental level. If you find that you cannot compose feedback that would be clear to the student, the problem may be that the learning goal and criteria themselves were not appropriate for that student.

SPECIFICITY

When feedback is too specific—for example, when the teacher copyedits a student's paper or supplies the correct answers to problems—the next-step work is already done for the student. A student could "fix" the work without having learned anything. Conversely, comments that are too general (e.g., "Add more") are not helpful. That middle level of generality in feedback we seek as students is, in fact, the most effective (Kluger & DeNisi, 1996). Giving examples in feedback can help, as long as students do not use examples as complete definitions of the criteria (Sadler, 1989) or think that their revisions need to exactly match your examples.

AMOUNT

You have choices about how much feedback to give—how many points to comment on and how much to say about each one. It is generally not effective to comment on everything possible. This would be overwhelming for most students and not helpful for even the most resilient. Rather, it is more effective to select the most important points the student should attend to in pursuit of their next steps toward a learning goal. Most often, the feedback should center on the success criteria (see Chapter 2) that will become the focus of the student's next steps in learning. Sadler (1989, p. 133) put it this way: "Which of the potential criteria are singled out for mention has less to do with what is detectable through the senses than with what is deemed to be *worth noticing*" (emphasis in original).

Once you have decided on what elements in the work need comment, use elaborated feedback on those points (Butler &

Winne, 1995; Mason & Bruning, 2001; Shute, 2008). Instead of simply "correcting" student work, describe what you see in the work and make a suggestion for how to improve it, but don't do the revising for the student. Effective, elaborated feedback should require students to think about what learning or understanding they are trying to demonstrate in their work and make revisions in the work to take it closer to meeting the criteria. If the teacher does this for the student, the student is deprived of this opportunity to learn. For example, rather than marking in a missing comma in a sentence, say, "There is a comma fault in this paragraph (or sentence, depending on how much scaffolding you want to provide). Find it and fix it."

Examples of Feedback Messages

We have often observed teachers drawing smiley faces or stars on a student's product or writing a complimentary comment such as "nice work." Using the feedback dimensions described above, the comment, "nice work," can be characterized as follows: the feedback is written; it focuses on a student's product, applies unknown criteria, is individually directed, and evaluative. Although it is hard to determine the impact of the comment on an individual student's learning, we can infer, based on what we know from research, that the impact is most likely to be minimal. Askew and Lodge (2000) would describe this type of feedback as "a gift" from the teacher to the student. It reflects a conception of learning in which the teacher is the expert who can knowledgeably critique the students' work. The primary focus of this type of feedback is evaluation. Evaluative feedback is also readily observed in nonverbal modes, all too common in the form of a teacher's disapproving facial expression.

Consider another example. A teacher comments on a student's table by writing in the student's science notebook: "Great description of the types of materials we are studying. Good properties to describe the materials: color, texture, and particle size. What properties have we discussed that are missing in your table to help you better differentiate and describe types of materials?" Using the dimensions previously described, we can analyze and characterize the comment as follows: written, focuses on a student's process, uses known criteria—the properties to describe material used in class. Further, it is individualized and evaluative but also descriptive. Although it is equally difficult to predict the eventual impact the comment will have on the student's learning, research strongly supports the expectation that it will have a stronger impact than the "nice work" comment.

It is important to note that the second feedback example somehow invites and opens a dialogue with the student. At least posing a question invites the student to respond. The student then can choose to review her work and improve her learning. Askew and Lodge (2000) refer to this feedback as forming "a loop." The feedback is constructed based on dialogues, or loops of information, in which the teacher and the student share the responsibility for a final product. This type of looping comment reflects a conception of learning that involves self-reflection or regulation of the learning process (e.g., learning strategies) and analyzing and transforming information. It involves another key characteristic: the teacher is a facilitator (rather than the giver) who can help the student to form connections, make sense of new meanings, and gain new insights. The teacher also learns new ways to facilitate students' learning and self-reflection. The primary focus of this type of looping comment is to "construct a way to move learning forward" (Tunstall & Gipps, 1996). This type of comment can also be presented orally, to an individual or to the class as a whole.

Instructional Moves as Feedback: What We Are Missing

Some research suggests that the weakest aspect of the formative assessment framework is teachers' use of feedback in response to the information collected (e.g., Black & Wiliam, 1998; Ruiz-Primo & Furtak, 2006, 2007; Ruiz-Primo, Li, Sands, Willis, & O'Brian, 2010). Heritage, Kim, Vendlinski, & Herman (2009) found that teachers could more easily use students' work to draw conclusions about students' understanding than to design the next instructional move. In many cases, the next instructional move after feedback should be to give students an opportunity to use it. This means, for example, allocating some lesson time for students to revise their work, perhaps giving them a structure to use, such as annotating their revisions with sticky notes to show where they used particular feedback suggestions.

Wylie and Lyon (2015) analyzed two years' worth of data from mathematics and science teachers participating in Keeping Learning on Track, a formative assessment professional development program designed to increase teachers' implementation of formative assessment practices and use of the resulting assessment information in a formative learning cycle. Overall, less than half (46%, p. 156) of teachers used the information for subsequent instructional moves, supporting Heritage and colleagues' (2009) conclusion that using formative assessment information is challenging for teachers. Also, disturbingly, a full 18% used formative assessment techniques in ways that rendered them not formative.

To use formative assessment information to decide on next instructional moves, teachers need to have deep pedagogical content knowledge (Baird, Hopfenbeck, Newton, Stobart, & Steen-Utheim, 2014; Bennett, 2011; Black, Wilson, & Yao, 2011; Heritage, 2013). Teachers need deep domain knowledge to interpret the student thinking represented in student work or student discourse. Then, they need a flexible repertoire of instructional moves that they can apply strategically based on their appraisal of the students' next steps in learning. Those instructional moves need to include multiple ways of representing the same concept and be student-centered, helping students take advantage of their own assessment information (Heitink, Van der Kleij, Veldkamp, Schildkamp, & Kippers, 2016).

This is a tall order. It is no wonder that many teachers do not use assessment information very well to design next instructional moves (Heritage et al., 2009; Ruiz-Primo, Kroog, & Sands, 2015; Wylie & Lyon, 2015). It is often the case that teachers use assessment information to identify students who need extra help, and what to re-teach, but not necessarily how to re-teach it (Goertz, Oláh, & Riggan, 2009). This is likely because teachers primarily use assessment data to draw conclusions about students' understanding of procedures and the correctness of their answers, not to understand their conceptual thinking (Oláh, Lawrence, & Riggan, 2010).

Oláh and her colleagues were studying teachers' feedback based on formal, large-scale interim/benchmark assessment. When focusing on informal formative assessment, the study by Ruiz-Primo et al. (2015) revealed, perhaps counter-intuitively, both mathematics and science teachers, on average, provided more feedback during whole-class instruction than when students were doing individual work. Across all instructional tasks observed during whole-class instruction, teachers responded to formative assessment information most frequently with statements (verbal feedback; mathematics, 19.2%; science, 33.3%), much less with instructional moves (mathematics, 6.9%; science, 3.6%). Furthermore, fewer teacher-student interactions were observed on tasks that involved individual student work (mathematics, 14.3%; science, 10.5%) than whole-class (mathematics, 44.7%; science, 46.6%). There was much variation by teacher.

It seems fair to us to conclude that the limited amount of research evidence available to date suggests that, for both formal and informal formative assessment, teachers' responses to the formative assessment evidence in student work are largely either absent, continuing with the lesson as planned, or simply procedural. Focused feedback comments are rare during lessons, and instructional moves are rarer still.

Deciding on the Next Instructional Move

In a previous section, we made the point that feedback comments should be based on the criteria for success students and teachers should have been sharing and using, and that the comments should identify the student's next step and not every possible step. Learning is incremental, and taking one step successfully is better than being overwhelmed and taking no steps at all (Covington, 1992).

A similar principle holds for feedback in the form of next instructional moves. The key is to decide what students should focus on next in order to take the next step in the formative learning cycle. For example, instead of simply observing that a student is having difficulty with carrying in two-digit addition and therefore assigning another set of similar problems, you should focus instruction on the student's particular difficulty. Is it understanding place value? Understanding the concept of tens and ones? Making the place value marks in the right place? Or, for example, instead of simply observing that a student can't solve problems involving the rotation and revolution of the planets, you need to focus instruction on students' particular misunderstandings. Do they not realize two motions happen at once? Do they not understand that planets tilt? Are they confusing planets turning around their own axes with planets following an orbital path? If your next instructional moves (explanations, activities) focus on the particular issue, the effectiveness of the formative learning cycle is maximized.

At the present time, our best advice is to target the smallest practicable instructional group, similar to the advice to give individual feedback when practical. However, differentiating instruction does not necessarily mean separate learning targets, lessons, and activities for every student. Often small-group work is not only feasible but effective, as students have a chance to work and construct meaning with their peers. Differentiated instruction can be the next instructional move (or, as Tomlinson (2014) calls it, "the bridge between today's lesson and tomorrow's"). In Tomlinson's (2014) formulation, feedback comments and next instructional moves work together, and both should be used in tandem. This advice echoes both the admonition in the previous section to make sure students have an immediate opportunity to use feedback—which amounts to a next instructional move—and with Ruiz-Primo and colleagues' (2015) observations that, in the infrequent classroom episodes where formative assessment is used effectively, teachers do use both comments and instructional moves together.

Finally, it is important to note that a next instructional move means a new learning target, a lesson-sized goal that students can aim for and understand as a next step toward their larger learning goal (Moss & Brookhart, 2012). That means students need to know what they are expecting to learn during this next bit of instruction, how they are going to learn it and what they will do to get evidence of how they are learning. They need to know what criteria for success to use to monitor and assess their own work as they go and how you, the teacher, will be assessing their work.

A Guide to Characterize Comments and Instructional Moves

In the previous section we described feedback characteristics that are well known in the literature. In this section we take another approach to think about feedback. We provide a guide for thinking about comments and instructional moves based on one of the fundamental characteristics of feedback already discussed—the function of the feedback.

The approach is presented in Table 3.1. The main distinction we make in presenting this guide is between *evaluative* and *descriptive* feedback. The arrow in the table indicates a continuum rather than a dichotomy. Sometimes, descriptive feedback involves an evaluative comment but the reverse is not true: evaluative feedback will not include a descriptive piece of information. We hope that the table supports understanding of why evaluative feedback does not help to improve students' learning or develop strategies to approach problems. We should consider evaluative feedback as feedback that may create more noise than true change (Perrenoud, 1998).

Facets of Students' Thinking and Feedback

As the first row of Table 3.1 indicates, feedback may affect three interrelated facets of students' thinking: motivation, attention, and self-regulatory processes.

Achievement Motivation

The quality of feedback helps shape student achievement motivation, a critical factor that we know affects students' learning. In turn, motivational process influences students' acquisition,

Table 3.1 Guide to Characterize Feedback for Both Comments and Instructional Moves

Facets	Evaluative ←→ Descriptive				
Motivation Attention Self-Regulation	Performance-Goal-Oriented Self or Product Hinders Self-Regulation		Learning-Goal-Oriented Process Supports Self-Regulation		
	E1	D1	D2	D3	D4
	Focuses on Judgments		*Focuses on Learning and Strategies*		
Teacher's Comments	Mentions correct/incorrect aspects of a product or student characteristic. Reflect approval or disapproval of what students do.	Focuses on student's progress; what has been attained; what standard has been met.	Describes the discrepancy (the error, the mismatch) between the learning goal and the current status. Focuses on aspects of the students' performance that need to be improved to achieve the learning goal; includes specifying expectations.	Focuses on how to proceed; how to improve or reach higher levels or how to compare previous and current levels. Critical difference with D2 is the language used; emphasis is on students' learning.	Focuses on co-appraisal; co-construction of criteria for success (e.g., helping students to develop strategies for error detection), share criteria that students can adopt to develop their own.

Student Participation	No Participation	No Participation	No Participation	Co-Participation	Co-Participation
Teacher's Instructional Moves	Provide correct answer with no explanation.	Makes physical changes in the classroom or temporal shifts in the discussion of topics without explanations to the students. Re-clarifies the task.	Models (reviews) how to solve the problem/task without the help of the student. Provides correct answer with an explanation.	Solves the problem/task with the help of the student(s). Helps to reinforce the strategies used in that type of problem/task.	Co-constructs with student(s) the bigger idea or the strategy that is the focus of a type of problem, something that goes beyond the tasks at hand.
Formative Use	Feedback that *Prevents* Formative Use		→		Feedback that *Facilitates* Formative Use
	Opportunities to revise are not provided.				Opportunities to revise are provided.

use, and transfer of knowledge and skills (Dweck, 1986, 2008). Achievement motivation, according to Dweck, involves two types of goals: (a) *learning goals* (also called mastery goals) are those for which students seek to increase their competence, to understand or master something new to them; and (b) *performance goals* are those for which students seek to gain positive judgments of their competence or to avoid negative judgments; students do not seek to learn, but rather they seek to look smart. Research in achievement motivation (Dweck, 2000) has made clear that when students genuinely pursue learning-oriented goals they look for challenging tasks, and they persist in the face of failure and obstacles. In sharp contrast, students who primarily pursue performance goals will avoid challenging tasks, will lack persistence or the resilience to overcome failure or obstacles. They look for easy and low-effort tasks that make them look smart.

The goals students pursue have even deeper implications (Dweck, 1986). Research has shown, for example, that students pursuing learning-oriented goals also believe that intelligence is not fixed, but malleable, and they have it within their power to increase their intelligence. If students are oriented mainly toward a performance goal, they tend to believe that intelligence is indeed fixed. If they do not perform well on a task they will attribute the performance to lack of intelligence, something they cannot change. When they face problems and failure, these students will show a maladaptive pattern that impedes their chances of overcoming failures and obstacles (e.g., "I am not smart," "I can't ever remember things," or "I am not good at this type of task"). Thus, successful or unsuccessful performance on instructional tasks is based less on the student's ability than on motivational factors.

Attention

The quality of the feedback may influence what students pay attention to: themselves, the product, or the process involved in understanding. The type of feedback centered on students' characteristics, on the "self," most likely will have little or no effect on learning, but as we have seen may have a negative effect on the students' motivation. Comments that focus only on students' personal characteristics (e.g., "you are so intelligent") or on students' products (e.g., "your table looks great" or "incomplete!") are not related explicitly to the learning goals being pursued or to the tasks in which students are engaged. Therefore, these types of feedback are limited in their impact on reducing the gap between where students are and where they can be (Kluger & DeNisi, 1996; James, Black, McCormick, & Pedder, 2007). These types of "feedback" include little information that can help the student to improve skills and knowledge, or to engage in the task with increased motivation. When we overemphasize performance goals in this way, we also drive out learning goals and foster student helplessness (e.g., "I can't do this type of task; I knew it!").

Feedback that focuses on the process underlying the task is more likely to affect students' learning and strategies. This type of feedback, however, must be descriptive and focus on different aspects of the student's performance: (a) describing what the student has accomplished, and/or what needs to be worked on or improved; and/or (b) making evident the process that the student needed to engage in to do the task; and/or (c) helping the student to compare previous and current achievements/performances.

We can say that the highest level of feedback is that which involves the student as a learner who can reflect on his or her own learning. It is feedback that helps the student make connections about what has been learned at any given point. For some (Askew & Lodge, 2000; James et al., 2007; Tunstall & Gipps, 1996), this type of feedback leads to a "dialogue" between teacher and student or among students. Not necessarily oral, this dialogue is evident in the type of written language that the teacher employs in her comment. It is a language that is less concerned about judgments (or an expert helping a novice), and more about facilitating the student's connections, learning, and strategies to monitor and direct herself—strategies to become a more autonomous learner.

Self-Regulation

By this point, we hope we have made clear that the quality of your comments to students does affect, in different ways, students' motivation and what they attend to about learning. An important goal of formative assessment, and indeed for some the ultimate goal (e.g., Allal, 2011; Askew & Lodge, 2000; James et al., 2007; Perrenoud, 1998; Sadler, 1989), is for students to be involved in their own assessment in a way that will cause them to reflect on where they are in their own learning, understand where they need to go, and decide what to do next. In other words, we should "place the work in the hands of the students" (James et al., 2007, p. 27) —students need to self-monitor and guide themselves toward achievement of the learning goal. For self-regulation to occur, as we have noted, it is important that the learning goals are clear, the students understand them (what learning should I pursue and for what purpose?), and the motivational processes are those that support learning-oriented goals (what are my opportunities for learning something new?).

Feedback that supports student self-regulation will help students become self-monitoring and self-directing and can ultimately improve performance on difficult tasks (Dweck, 2000). Kluger and DeNisi (1996) have suggested that feedback with the potential to influence self-regulation may be the most effective type of feedback. Teacher comments that encourage students to reflect on skills they are developing can help those students to become "metacognitively wiser" (Askew & Lodge, 2000). According to Perrenoud (1998), feedback that is limited to pointing out errors will have the weakest impact on self-regulation.

Student Participation

As we move toward the right side of Table 3.1, the types of feedback described involve the student as more than a passive learner, but rather, as the agent in charge of his or her own learning. In this respect, feedback provides information that helps students to improve their learning strategies and their learning, because it helps them to develop motivation to learn, attend to the most essential aspects of tasks, and improve their self-regulation skills. The table also shows how most of the instructional moves involve the use of comments that have the potential to generate a dialogue with students.

Providing Students an Opportunity to Use Feedback

Designing opportunities for students to use feedback bridges the gap between comment feedback and next steps in instruction. Simply returning an assignment with comments on it to students does not guarantee, or even necessarily encourage, students' use of the feedback to improve their work or to further their learning. In fact, providing students an opportunity to use feedback can work to equalize opportunity for learning. Research suggests that high-achieving students will use any piece of information they can get to improve their work and their learning (Brookhart, 2001). Providing lesson time and scaffolding as needed for students to use feedback can extend some of these benefits to all students. When teachers give students time to work with the feedback they receive, students perceive that feedback as positive and feel their learning is enhanced (Gamlem & Smith, 2013; Pokorny & Pickford, 2010).

Skillful teachers can structure immediate opportunities for students to use feedback. Heritage and Heritage (2013) analyzed videos of two teacher-student interactions in one fifth-grade class to show that oral feedback in the form of pedagogic questioning is effective feedback that blurs the line between comments and instructional moves. As the students engaged in dialogue with the teacher they were using the feedback for learning on the spot. Feedback in the form of dialogue with students, based on pedagogic questions, can take place within the student's zone of proximal development (Vygotsky, 1978) and feed learning forward.

Closing Comments

Comments and instructional moves can both be considered types of feedback if they are deeply tied to criteria for learning and given in response to formative assessment evidence gleaned from student work. They often can and should be used together. In this chapter, we have examined the research for how to do this effectively, noting that the body of research on feedback comments is much larger than the body of research on next instructional moves, and provided examples in practice. Further, taking next instructional moves has been found to be difficult for many teachers. In the next chapter we will look more closely at the conditions for effective teachers' feedback.

References

Askew, S., & Lodge, S. (2000). Gifts, ping-pong and loops—linking feedback and learning. In S. Askew (Ed.), *Feedback for learning* (pp. 17–32). New York, NY: Routledge.

Baird, J., Hopfenbeck, T. N., Newton, P., Stobart, G., & Steen-Utheim, A. T. (2014). *State of the field review: Assessment and learning.* Oslo: Knowledge Center for Education.

Bangert-Drowns, R. L., Kulik, C-L., Kulik, J. A., & Morgan, M. T. (1991). The instructional effect of feedback in test-like events. *Review of Educational Research*, *61*(2), 213–238.

Bennett, R. E. (2011). Formative assessment: A critical review. *Assessment in Education: Principles, Policy & Practice*, *18*(1), 5–25.

Black, P., & Wiliam, D. (1998). Assessment and classroom learning. *Assessment in Education: Principles, Policy, & Practice*, *5*(1), 7–74.

Black, P., Wilson, M., & Yao, S-Y. (2011). Road maps for learning: A guide to the navigation of learning progressions. *Measurement: Interdisciplinary Research and Perspectives*, *9*(2–3), 71–123.

Bloom, B. S. (1984). The 2 sigma problem: The search for methods of group instruction as effective as one-to-one tutoring. *Educational Researcher*, *13*(6), 4–16.

Boaler, J. (2016). *Mathematical mindset: Unleashing students' potential through creative math, inspiring messages, and innovative teaching.* San Francisco: Jossey-Bass.

Brookhart, S. M. (2001). Successful students' formative and summative use of assessment information. *Assessment in Education*, *8*, 153–169.

Brookhart, S. M. (2017). *How to give effective feedback to your students* (2nd ed.). Alexandria, VA: ASCD.

Butler, D. L., & Winne, P. H. (1995). Feedback and self-regulated learning: A theoretical synthesis. *Review of Educational Research*, *65*, 245–281.

Covington, M. V. (1992). *Making the grade: A self-worth perspective on motivation and school reform*. Cambridge: Cambridge University Press.

Crooks, T. J. (1988). The impact of classroom evaluation practices on students. *Review of Educational Research, 58*, 438–481.

Deci, E. L., & Ryan, R. M. (1985). *Intrinsic motivation and self-determination in human behavior*. New York: Plenum.

Dweck, C. S. (1986). Motivational processes affecting learning. *American Psychologists, 41*(10), 1040–1048.

Dweck, C. S. (2000). *Self-theories: Their role in motivation, personality, and development*. New York: Psychology Press.

Dweck, C. S. (2008). *Mindset. The new psychology of success*. New York, NY: Ballantine Books Trade Paperback Edition.

Gamlem, S. M., & Smith, K. (2013). Student perceptions of classroom feedback. *Assessment in Education: Principles, Policy and Practice, 20*, 150–169.

Goertz, M. E., Oláh, L. N., & Riggan, M. (2009, December). *From testing to teaching: The use of interim assessments in classroom instruction*. CPRE Policy Brief RB-51. Graduate School of Education, University of Pennsylvania.

Hargreaves, E., McCallum, B., & Gipps, C. (2000). Teacher feedback strategies in primary classrooms—new evidence. In S. Askew (Ed.), *Feedback for learning* (pp. 34–43). New York: Routledge.

Hattie, J. A. C. (2009). *Visible learning: A synthesis of over 800 meta-analyses relating to achievement*. London: Routledge.

Hattie, J. A. C., & Timperley, H. (2007). The power of feedback. *Review of Educational Research, 77*(1), 81–112.

Heitink, M. C., Van der Kleij, F. M., Veldkamp, B. P., Schildkamp, K., & Kippers, W. B. (2016). A systematic review of prerequisites for implementing assessment for learning in classroom practice. *Educational Research Review, 17*, 50–62.

Heritage, M. (2013). *Formative assessment in practice: A process of inquiry and action*. Cambridge, MA: Harvard Education Press.

Heritage, M., & Heritage, J. (2013). Teacher questioning: The epicenter of instruction and assessment. *Applied Measurement in Education, 26*, 176–190.

Heritage, M., Kim, J., Vendlinski, T., & Herman, J. (2009). From evidence to action: A seamless process in formative assessment? *Educational Measurement: Issues and Practice, 28*(3), 24–31.

James, M., Black, P., McCormick, R., & Pedder, D. (2007). Promoting learning how to learn through assessment for learning. In M. James,

R. McCormick, P. Black, P. Carmichael, M-J, Drummond, A. Fox, J. MacBeath, B. Marshall, D. Pedder, R. Procter, S. Swaffield, J. Swann, & D. Wiliam. (Eds.), *Improving learning how to learn: Classrooms, schools, and network* (pp. 21–42). New York, NY: Routledge.

Johnston, P. H. (2004). *Choice words: How our language affects children's learning.* Portland, ME: Stenhouse.

Kluger, A. N., & DeNisi, A. (1996). The effects of feedback interventions on performance: A historical review, a meta-analysis, and a preliminary feedback intervention theory. *Psychological Bulletin, 119,* 254–284.

Koenka, A., Moshontz, H., Atkinson, K. M., Sanchez, C. E., & Cooper, H. (2016, April). *The impact of grades, comments, and no feedback on academic achievement: A meta-analysis.* Paper presented at the American Educational Research Association, Washington, DC.

Kroog, H. I., Ruiz-Primo, M. A., & Sands, D. (2014). *Understanding the interplay between the cultural context of classrooms and formative assessment.* Paper presented at the annual meeting of the American Educational Research Association, Philadelphia, PA.

Mason, B. J., & Bruning, R. (2001). *Providing feedback in computer-based instruction: What the research tells us.* University of Nebraska-Lincoln. Retrieved from http://dwb.unl.edu/Edit/MB/MasonBruning.html

Minstrell, J., Anderson, R., & Li, M. (2009). *Assessing teacher competency in formative assessment.* Annual Report to the National Science Foundation. Alexandria, VA: National Science Foundation.

Mory, E. H. (2004). Feedback research revisited. In D. Jonassen (Ed.), *Handbook of research on educational communications and technology* (pp. 745–783). Mahwah, NJ: Lawrence Erlbaum.

Moss, C. M., & Brookhart, S. M. (2012). *Learning targets: Helping students aim for understanding in today's lesson.* Alexandria, VA: ASCD.

Oláh, L. N., Lawrence, N. R., & Riggan, M. (2010). Learning to learn from benchmark assessment data: How teachers analyze results. *Peabody Journal of Education, 85,* 226–245.

Ormrod, J. E. (2014). *Educational psychology: Developing learners* (8th ed.). Boston: Pearson.

Perrenoud, P. (1998). From formative evaluation to a controlled regulation of learning process. Towards a wider conceptual field. *Assessment in Education: Principles, Policy, & Practice, 5*(1), 85–102.

Pokorny, H., & Pickford, P. (2010). Complexity, cues, and relationships: Student perceptions of feedback. *Active Learning in Higher Education, 11,* 21–30.

Reeve, J. (2002). Self-determination theory applied to educational settings. In E. L. Deci & R. M. Ryan (Eds.), *Handbook of self-determination research* (pp. 183–203). Rochester, NY: University of Rochester Press.

Ruiz-Primo, M. A., & Furtak, E. M. (2006). Informal formative assessment and scientific inquiry: Exploring teachers' practices and student learning. *Educational Assessment, 11*(3–4), 205–235.

Ruiz-Primo, M. A., & Furtak, E. M. (2007). Exploring teachers' informal formative assessment practices and students' understanding in the context of scientific inquiry. *Journal of Research in Science Teaching, 44*(1), 57–84.

Ruiz-Primo, M. A., Kroog, H., & Sands, D. I. (2015, August). *Teachers' judgments on-the-fly: Teachers' response patterns in the context of informal formative assessment.* Paper presented at the EARLI Biennial Conference, Limassol, Cyprus.

Ruiz-Primo, M. A., & Li, M. (2004). On the use of students' science notebooks as an assessment tool. *Studies in Educational Evaluation, 30,* 61–85.

Ruiz-Primo, M. A., & Li, M. (2013). Analyzing teachers' feedback practices in response to students' work in science classrooms. Special Issue on Using Evidence to Take Action: Strategies Teachers Use to Deconstruct Student Work. *Applied Measurement in Education, 26*(3), 163–175.

Ruiz-Primo, M. A., Li, M., Sands, D., Willis, K., & O'Brian, J. (2010, April). *Developing and evaluating instructionally sensitive assessments.* Paper presented at the American Educational Research Association Annual Meeting. Denver, CO.

Sadler, D. R. (1989). Formative assessment and the design of instructional systems. *Instructional Science, 18,* 119–144.

Shute, V. J. (2008). Focus on formative feedback. *Review of Educational Research, 78*(1), 153–189.

Stiggins, R. J., & Conklin, N. F. (1992). *In teachers' hands: Investigating the practices of classroom assessment.* Albany, NY: SUNY Press.

Tomlinson, C. A. (2014). The bridge between today's lesson and tomorrow's. *Educational Leadership, 71*(6), 10–14.

Tunstall, P., & Gipps, C. (1996). Teacher feedback to young children in formative assessment: A typology. *British Educational Research Journal, 22*(4), 389–404.

Van der Kleij, F. M., Feskens, R. C. W., & Eggen, T. J. H. M. (2015). Effects of feedback in a computer-based learning environment on students' learning outcomes: A meta-analysis. *Review of Educational Research, 85*(4), 475–511.

Vygotsky, L. S. (1978). *Mind and society: The development of higher mental processes*. Cambridge, MA: Harvard University Press.

Wylie, E. C., & Lyon, C. J. (2015). The fidelity of formative assessment implementation: Issues of breadth and quality. *Assessment in Education: Principles, Policy and Practice, 22,* 140–160.

4

Implementing Effective Feedback
Some Challenges and Some Solutions

This chapter looks at the challenges that you may face when implementing the four formative assessments activities involved in feedback episodes: (a) sharing and clarifying learning goals, expectations, and criteria with students; (b) gathering information critical to determining where students are in their learning; (c) analyzing and meaningfully interpreting the information to make it usable for yourself and your students; and (d) acting upon or using the information by directly providing or facilitating the provision of feedback that will support the students' learning. We organize the discussion around the formative assessments activities and the formality with which formative assessment can happen. That is, we discuss the challenges and the strategies that can help reduce them by considering formal and informal formative assessment contexts. We begin by reviewing the main differences between formal and informal formative assessment. Then we discuss the challenges in implementing effective feedback, by formative assessment activity. We use information from studies to provide empirical evidence about the challenges, and we provide some strategies that can considerably lessen the challenges and improve the effectiveness of feedback.

Informal and Formal Formative Assessment

As we mentioned in an earlier chapter, we distinguish between informal and formal formative assessment. The major difference between formal formative assessment (FFA) and informal formal assessment (IFA) is the degree of formality that teachers apply when gathering information about students' learning, as well as the level of formality with which they respond to students based on their interpretation of the collected information (on-the-fly or more formally). FFA helps you to know where *every student is* with respect to critical knowledge or skills that are important for building understanding and achieving the unit's learning goals. IFA helps you to know where *some* students are in a continuous manner.

Both IFA and FFA yield information on which to base decisions about responding appropriately to students' needs. When teachers have a chance to talk with almost all the students as they work independently, or when teachers give the class a test, then it may be reasonable to say that the information they are gathering is about almost all the students. The resulting teacher decisions are well-informed decisions. However, if teachers make instructional decisions based on responses from only a few students (often the more able), such as typically occurs during a class discussion, teacher inferences will be based on a small student sample and the decisions made can be inappropriate. In other words, certainty about the inferences we make about what students know and can do and where they are in their learning may vary depending on whether the inferences are based on a *sample* of a few students or *all* the students. It is also important to keep in mind that you have the option and the power to pay attention to and include all of the students in class interactions: not only the eager hand-raisers, but, more important, those who do not volunteer to participate.

Three characteristics guide classroom work and are intimately related to the nature of formative assessment and feedback: instructional modes, sources used to gather information from students, and the interplay between formal and informal formative assessment.

Instructional Modes

All instruction takes place within a context (Alexander, 2008). In the framework introduced in Chapter 1, we discussed routines, norms, and *instructional modes* (or ways in which students are organized) as part of this context. In the DEMFAP project the researchers (Ruiz-Primo, Iverson, & Sands, 2013; Ruiz-Primo, Kroog, & Sands, 2015) observed that classroom instruction occurred in three modes: whole class, small groups/pairs, or individually. These structures offer varying opportunities to support students' learning. Teachers engage in FFA in whole-class mode when they give a quiz or a test or when they give all students the same handout to work on. The teacher then can analyze and interpret the information collected using the students' products and responses (e.g., determine the percentage of students who correctly answered each question in a quiz) and act on the information collected (e.g., model how to approach a certain type of problem). However, there is more to whole-class formative assessment than giving quizzes. Whole-class teaching offers an opportunity to have revealing discussions with students. For example, the teacher and students can discuss and analyze questions that produce a low percentage of correct responses. Alexander (2008) asserts that a critical task for teachers is to facilitate learning by creating and using opportunities to interact with students. In fact, whole-class discussions have been considered one of the most powerful tools, offering many possibilities for enhancing student learning using IFA (Alexander, 2008; Black, Wilson, & Yao, 2011).

Similarly, individual interactions with students present opportunities to address each student's specific needs. Ruiz-Primo et al. (2015) observed that teachers deemed effective at formative assessment used 5- to 10-minute individual work tasks with a large percentage of their students to provide feedback at the individual level. With almost every student, pair of students, or small group, they stopped to question, observe, and/or listen to students, and then followed with some type of helpful feedback, using efficient strategies. In one particularly efficient practice, as teachers walked around observing how students were working, they left sticky notes with brief comments on top of the students' papers, a very efficient strategy to provide individual feedback in response to individual needs (O'Brian, 2013).

Unfortunately, too often, teachers treat individual work solely as a way to keep students on track, which means they miss many opportunities to encourage and stimulate students to improve their learning. Teachers should view the different instructional modes as opportunities to gather information, analyze and interpret that information (whether on-the-fly or not), and then respond to students' needs in different ways and with varying degrees of formality.

Sources Used to Gather Evidence

On any given day, there are multiple opportunities to informally gather evidence about students' learning. Listening, observing, and asking questions become critical tools for *informally* gathering evidence about student learning. For example, when a student asks a question indicating confusion about something, we can treat the occasion as an opportunity to *understand the student's thinking* more fully and then *take action* that will help move the student forward (i.e., provide a comment, another question, or make an instructional move such as providing additional work). Observing or listening to students while they are working is a staple of teaching. Less common, however, is observing and listening to students *interpretatively* for the purpose of gaining insights into students' thinking. With an *interpretative* state of mind (Davis, 1997) teachers are ready to gather the desired information and take the next step. Only by maintaining this state of mind is it possible *to notice*—that is, to attend, interpret, and decide what to do next (Jacobs, Lamb, & Philipp, 2010).

Tasks used to gather evidence *formally* differ from those used in IFA. We believe that FFA is more than quizzes or tests embedded in a unit. Rather, any task that all (or almost all) of the students respond to or work on is a potential source for gathering information in a formal manner (e.g., a handout with a set of problems or a homework assignment). If tasks are thoughtfully developed, they can help to make student's thinking explicit, can help teachers more easily identify problems students are having, and they also should facilitate making decisions about next steps.

The Interplay Between Informal and Formal Formative Assessment

We view informal and formal formative assessment as a continuum. At any point on this informal-to-formal continuum the assessment process includes *gathering*, *interpreting*, and *acting* upon the evidence collected, all *guided by a particular goal* that we want students to achieve (Ruiz-Primo, 2010). Informal assessment at one end of the formative assessment continuum may be completely implicit. For example, during a class conversation when a teacher noticed that students "looked perplexed and confused," she rephrased what she had just said but without any obvious justification (Jordan & Putz, 2004). In this situation, the teacher relied on the students' facial gestures as a source of evidence to infer that the students did not fully understand what she was saying, so she rephrased to clarify the intended message.

At the other end of the continuum, formal assessment, what is implicit gradually becomes explicit. In everyday practice, at the formal end of the continuum, when the assessment message is shared (e.g., teachers and students discuss responses on a quiz), it is inevitable that there will be opportunities to interact with the students. If students simply receive the results of their test or a quiz, with no follow-up discussion, then a learning opportunity is lost. This means that informal formative assessment should be embedded in the discussion of the results of a formal formative assessment episode; otherwise, the episode is incomplete. This leads to our emphasis on an interplay between the formal and informal nature of formative assessment.

Formative Assessment Activities: Challenges and Strategies to Approach Them

We cannot view feedback only as how we act in response to students. Effective feedback is integral to quality formative assessment, and should therefore be a guiding consideration in every formative assessment activity: clarifying learning goals, expectations, and criteria; gathering information about students' learning, analyzing and interpreting information, and acting on the information collected. Still, implementing effective feedback is challenging. We use these activities as organizers in this section. Each starts with empirical evidence about the practices observed in the classroom and what is problematic about them. Then we provide some strategies to help improve the implementation of effective feedback practices.

Clarifying Learning Goals, Expectations, and Criteria

Ruiz-Primo and Kroog (2016) found that in about 70% of the 420 days observed during the DEMFAP project, teachers did not provide any learning goals, expectations, or success criteria to students. Furthermore, teachers did not mention the purpose of what students were doing (the activity/task purpose) in 65% of the 1,084 tasks observed in mathematics classes, and in 57% of the 895 tasks observed in science classes.

We cannot take for granted that students know why they are doing something. Students need help to understand the big picture and how what they do every day is connected. As Mary White (1971) wrote about learning goals and sailing destinations: "imagine oneself on a ship sailing across the unknown sea, to an unknown destination. An adult would be desperate to know where he is going. But a child only knows he is going to the school" (p. 340). Using White's analogy, we can say, based on the information reported by Ruiz-Primo and Kroog (2016), that in the majority of the days observed students did not have a "journey's end," and that in the majority of the instructional activities students did in their classroom were completed with an "unknown destination."

Indeed, one reason that formative assessment may not work as well as we would like is that the learning goals and success criteria teachers share with the students are usually ambiguous and vague (Nebelsick-Gullet, Hamen Farrar, Huff, & Packman, 2013). Only when you fully understand the role that each instructional activity plays in achieving a learning goal can you convey to your students its purpose and importance. But your job does not end there. It is also essential that you know whether your students understand it, and if they don't, which strategies to use to help them understand it, as well as helping them to set their own learning goals.

Thus, a critical part of your role as a teacher is to make sure that your students actually know why they are doing what they are doing. This can be readily incorporated in a teacher's instructional routines. It can take less than a minute, for example, to explain to students the purpose of a task, how it connects with past or future activities, and/or expectations for what the students should pay attention to. These kinds of messages can make the difference between students focusing solely on what they need to complete and concentrating on learning from a task and discovering connections that might otherwise be missed. If students are uncertain about why they are doing something, they should ask questions about the assignment or project. Moreover, such latitude and expectations can motivate students to apply their best efforts when carrying out a task.

Also, when you keep in mind the most important things students need to learn, you can streamline your methods for gathering information. Clear learning goals make it possible to develop, select, and/or adapt instructional activities as a coherent set of tasks that can be arranged in ways that will demonstrate how students are improving. That is, the design and analysis of tasks should be goal-oriented, with the aim of activating students' knowledge and skills in ways that will lead them to use it for improving their learning and strategies. The learning experience is enhanced and feedback is more focused and appropriate when both teachers and students are fully aware not only of *what* is to be learned but also *how* each task contributes to the overall goal of the unit, module, or chapter.

As mentioned in Chapter 2, understanding what you teach requires more than being familiar with the sequence of instructional activities in a unit, a topic, or a chapter. It involves distinguishing between what is and is not critical for your students' learning. It involves understanding why something comes first and something else comes later. A full grasp of what you teach involves knowing how students' understanding becomes more sophisticated as instruction unfolds and what instructional activities students need to be engaged with to develop and practice the necessary knowledge and skills. If you are clear about what critical blocks of knowledge and skills are to be developed, which blocks of knowledge are pre-requisites for others, and how they are related, it becomes easier to identify specific aspects of the students' performance to focus on as instruction unfolds. Sztajn and colleagues (2012) contend that if teachers understand the continuum (called by them *learning trajectories*) of how students develop their thinking and become more proficient, teachers can better examine the demands of a task "not solely in relation to content following the logic of the discipline but as relations between tasks and students, following the logic of the learner" (p. 150).

Understanding the learning goals provides you with the *interpretative* state of mind, mentioned earlier, that gives you the capabilities to attend, notice, and interpret the relevant aspects of what students say, do, write, or make and to respond to this noticing by facilitating or providing the most focused, meaningful, and actionable feedback (Davis, 1997; Heritage, 2013; Jacobs, Lamb, & Philipp, 2010).

Gathering Evidence of Student Learning

Any task in which students engage is a potential source of information about where they are in their learning. Gathering information about students' learning then is about designing and selecting tasks that can elicit critical information from students. Designing or selecting appropriate task is, without a question, challenging; whether we think about tasks for FFA or IFA. For example, as part of the DEMFAP project (Ruiz-Primo & Sands, 2009), 3,459 students' products (artifacts) were collected during the 420 days that teachers were observed. An analysis of these artifacts conducted by Kroog, King Hess, and Ruiz-Primo (2016) found that in 52% of these artifacts, the tasks students were asked to engage with were designed to practice something. More importantly, only 14% of the work that teachers graded was designed to make students' thinking explicit (e.g., by eliciting potential students' naïve conceptions, mistakes, misapplications, and/or common errors).

In a study conducted with 58 teachers observed on two occasions (except for two teachers who were observed only on one occasion), Ruiz-Primo and Kroog (2017) analyzed the informal formative assessment practices in whole-class instructional mode. The analysis of the 114 observations focused on the three aspects: the strategies used by teachers to gather information, whether the students' responses made their thinking explicit, and the strategies used by teachers to respond to students' needs. The combination of the strategies observed in these three aspects lead to different quality profiles. These researchers found that in 49% of the mathematics profiles and in 32% of the science profiles identified, teachers asked fact-based questions as a strategy to gather information. These types of questions, in most cases, led to students' responses that did not reflect their thinking. In turn, teachers provided feedback that was rather general or did nothing at all. Identifying and asking the right questions is not as easy as we may think. Furthermore, in 53% and 44% of the profiles observed in the mathematics and science classrooms, respectively, students' thinking was not explicit; that is, their responses were such that it was hard to know whether they understood the topic at hand.

Thinking About Tasks to Gather Information

Well-designed tasks will (a) make students' thinking explicit, (b) signal students what is important to learn, (c) help you identify and understand the critical problems you need to focus on, (c) facilitate analysis and the interpretation of students' responses to the task, and (d) most likely, lead to feedback that is focused and will directly promote self-regulation and learning.

Designing effective instructional tasks in an appropriate sequence is part of the complexity of creating quality learning experiences (Bennett, Desforges, Cockburn, & Wilkinson, 1984; Kennewell, 2001; Marshall, Carmichael, & Drummond, 2007; Perrenoud, 1998). Good instructional tasks should allow tracing students' learning progress. With clear learning goals it is possible to order the instructional tasks to show how students are gaining a more in-depth understanding of a critical/core idea. We start by thinking about what we want students to be able to know and do at the end of a unit, then work backward and think about how each activity (or task) contributes to those goals.

MAKING STUDENTS' THINKING EXPLICIT

Torrance and Pryor (2001) proposed two types of tasks (or assessments, in their terms): (a) *Convergent tasks* that focus on determining *that* the student knows or understands something or whether the student can complete something that is pre-determined. These are pseudo-open tasks, and for these authors this type of task involves assessment *of* the student *by* the teacher. (b) *Divergent tasks* focus on exploring in-depth *what* the students know, understand, and can do. These tasks are open, relevant, and allow for more diversity in students' responses. Therefore, there is space for the teacher to facilitate students' learning and to create bridges to close the gap between where students are and where they should be. Divergent tasks are oriented more toward the future development of the student's learning rather than toward evaluating current achievement. Divergent tasks are expected to make students' thinking more explicit than convergent tasks.

How will you know that a task is making students' thinking explicit? In the context of IFA, questions that can lead to understanding student thinking are those that begin with "Why does . . . ?"; "How would you . . . ?"; "Could you explain . . . ?"; "Why do you think . . . ?"; "Why is _____ an example of _____?"; "Why is _____ and not _____?" Such probing questions can help to develop dialogical interactions (Stobart, 2014). Questions like these are consistent with the idea of divergent tasks. The most informative questions ask students to explain their answers, elaborate on their responses, or provide information about how they come to have certain ideas. In addition, sometimes we ask multiple questions with increasingly narrow focus, which can help us hone in on the source of students' thinking or confusion and therefore, provide the most appropriate and helpful feedback. The questions we ask and the interpretation of the students' responses should be based on the learning goal.

If you can identify the issues that students are struggling with, by observing them while they work on the task or by observing and analyzing their responses, then the task is making students' thinking explicit. This kind of quick look at how students are approaching a task will give you an idea of where individual students are, and will help you decide which students need an individual conversation or whether a whole-class discussion would be appropriate. For example, Ruiz-Primo et al. (2015) observed teachers seemingly casually walking among the tables where pairs of students were working and being able to quickly identify who was having a problem and with what. The teachers offered careful comments or implemented an instructional move in a quick and efficient manner. In other words, they knew what to look for "on-the-fly." If teachers do not know what they are looking for, then the task will not be helpful even if it is making students' thinking explicit.

In the context of FFA, there is always the option to design multiple-choice questions where the distractors represent common students' misconceptions that can signal the level of students' understanding. This information helps you decide what to do next to improve the students' learning (see Briggs, Alonzo, Schwab, & Wilson, 2006).

TASK PURPOSES AND LEVELS OF DIFFICULTY

When you design or select tasks, keep in mind that the purpose of the task will help you determine that task's demands. Ask yourself questions such as: Is the purpose of the task to introduce students to new ideas and concepts, or have students look at familiar materials in a different manner, or use familiar concepts or knowledge in unfamiliar contexts? Is the purpose of the task to have students practice new skills, fine-tuning them to become automatic processes, or is the purpose to have students to return to knowledge or skills that have not been used recently but are required for new learning?

We mentioned the study in which a good number of artifacts focused on practice tasks, without clarity of *what* exactly is being practiced. Practice is only productive when it is *deliberate* (Ericsson, 1996; Ericsson, Krampe, & Tesch-Römer, 1993), or as Syed (2010) says, *purposeful*. Research on how expertise develops shows that useful practice focuses on *exactly what we are not good at* (Colvin, 2008; Ericsson, 1996; Ericsson et al., 1993). Furthermore, through practice, teachers (like coaches), should notice what specifically is not still right and focus with students on that exact aspect. Repetition for repetition's sake is not helpful. Practicing *appropriately* is what matters. The artifacts collected in the DEMFAP project showed that although all the questions given to students addressed the topic at hand, it was difficult to identify immediately the purpose for which students were practicing something.

Deliberate practice, on the other hand, is designed to improve performance by pushing students a bit beyond their current level of understanding or skill. Such tasks are cognitively more demanding. They allow students to see an angle of a problem they had not noticed before; or they add elements not introduced before and which may be even unknown to them. These types of tasks fall into what is called the *learning zone* (term coined by Noel Tichy as cited by Colvin, 2008). Naturally, because of their novelty, students are likely to make more mistakes in completing tasks in the learning zone than in completing more tasks that are more familiar to them. These tasks provide a great opportunity for teachers to treat error in ways that lead to improving students' learning, if they are discussed properly. As we mentioned, each error a student makes is an opportunity for the student to grow, but *only if* the feedback helps the student to see connections the student did not see before. Feedback is the critical factor for improving performance in tasks that are in the learning zone. If students do not experience any improvement they may stop caring and not persevere in their efforts to complete tasks (Colvin, 2008).

In the DEMFAP project (Ruiz-Primo & Sands, 2009) one of the teachers prepared with anticipation three types of mathematics problems: easy, medium, and difficult ones. Some days she began the warm-up activities by asking her students: "What type of problem would you like to start with, an easy, a medium, or a hard one?" More than once, students voted for the hard one, despite the risk of making errors. Because errors in this class had been welcome since the first day of the school year, students had become accustomed to learning from their mistakes. Many studies of expert performance in the arts and sciences, sports, and games (see Ericsson, 1996) have shown that taking risks that may involve failure is an essential part of improving performance, rather than staying in a "routine of success." Tichy (as cited by Colvin, 2008) called this routine of success the *comfort zone*—that is, working on something that most of the students can already do easily. If you engage students only in tasks situated in their comfort zone, they will remain at that level of skills and be unlikely to improve their performance (Colvin, 2008; Stobart, 2014). You are also unlikely to get evidence upon which to base constructive feedback.

Tichy (as cited by Colvin, 2008) proposed yet another zone, the *panic zone*. Tasks in this zone are so hard that students do not even know how to approach them, which of course leads to a decline in their motivation and engagement. Obviously, you want to avoid using tasks that put students in the panic zone.

Tasks in the learning zone offer invaluable opportunities to provide feedback that can improve students' performance. These tasks should be created to overcome gaps, to apply what has been learned, and to deepen fluency with key concepts, procedures, or skills. In other words, good instructional tasks promote conceptual understanding and the development of thinking, reasoning, and problem-solving skills (Doyle, 1983). Tasks in the learning zone should involve *productive struggle*; they should engage and challenge students to think about and wrestle with ideas/concepts/processes critical to the topic they are learning (Hiebert & Grouws, 2007). *Struggle* means that students work to make sense of or figure out something "that is not immediately apparent" (Hiebert & Grouws, 2007, p. 387). Tasks in the learning zone can support productive whole-class discussion in which students can share strategies, focus on meaning making, and improve their understanding (Cartier, Smith, Stein, & Ross, 2013).

To design or select instructional tasks at the right level of difficulty you need to be aware of how students' knowledge develops over the span of the unit/topic/chapter, and identify the critical aspects on which they will focus their attention. That is, teachers need to understand how students' knowledge of the concepts, topics, and procedures that are the focus of instruction will develop over time (see Chapter 2).

THE ROLE OF ANTICIPATING STUDENTS' RESPONSES

Designing or selecting high-quality questions and tasks that make students' thinking explicit is linked to *anticipating students' likely responses* (both correct and incorrect) (Stein, Grover, & Henningsen, 1996; Stein, Engle, Smith, & Hughes, 2008). This supports proactive thinking about the different types of potential feedback that can help students improve their learning. Potential feedback is often identified as you engage in responding to the tasks (Stein et al., 2008). A good rule to keep in mind is: Never give a task or assignment to students that involves something you have not worked on before. Anticipate what errors students are likely to make and the misconceptions they may have, and then prepare questions and instructional moves that can help students to focus on critical aspects of the tasks they are given. Anticipating is not about identifying which student responses will be correct or incorrect. Rather, it is about sorting out the strategies that students can use, how these strategies relate to students' interpretations of a problem, and how these strategies relate to the relevant disciplinary concepts, representations, procedures, and practices (Stein et al., 2008). More importantly, anticipating helps teachers to develop an interpretative state of mind and to be prepared to provide a more appropriate, robust, and meaningful feedback, either orally or using instructional moves.

Anticipating allows for *contingent planning*, which serves to identify different paths of action that teachers can take depending on the students' responses (Threlfall, 2005). Contingent planning requires pre-planned feedback episodes because it requires teachers to predict what kind of student responses and contingent (hence the name) plans for the next steps will be appropriate. It should focus not only on content issues, but also on self-regulation. Feedback targeting meta-cognition should emphasize helping students to strategically plan how to approach the task at hand, monitoring their own understanding of the task, self-assessing and self-correcting their performance as the task is completed, and evaluating progress toward completion of the task (Hattie, Fisher, & Frey, 2016).

THE IMPORTANCE OF HOW TASKS ARE IMPLEMENTED

In most cases, teachers determine the setting (e.g., availability of time, some tools or procedures for students to use, the instructional mode) that will guide how students will engage with the instructional tasks. The way tasks are implemented may support or inhibit thoughtful learning. Too much control, for example, may lead students to feel that they cannot make mistakes, reflect on, or talk about their work and performance. In this sense, implementation of tasks becomes "foreign to the idea of learning"—that is, the instructional task is not engaging students' thinking processes, which should, in fact, be at the center of the task. "Thus, teachers will say of some pupils: they are active, they seem interested, they ask questions, they enter into dialogue, they seem to be learning, but the next day, there is nothing left" (Perrenoud, 1998, p. 89).

Research has shown that even if the characteristics of a task allow for productive struggle, implementation can weaken the original cognitive demands of the task (Cartier et al., 2013; Perrenoud, 1998; Stein et al., 2008; Stein et al., 1996). For example, as students are working, you may inadvertently discourage student efforts. Sometimes, in an effort to be helpful, teachers give students inappropriate scaffolding (e.g., directing a student to a certain strategy or supplying information in a task designed to help students work out their own strategies and locate information). Also, during the discussion of a task, you may insufficiently highlight the different strategies students use and how those strategies are related to different ways of understanding the concept at hand. As a result, students may miss opportunities to make important connections among their different strategies and ideas. Another example of lost opportunity is paying attention to the wrong aspect of the students' responses (e.g., neatness rather than content of students' explanations or how nicely they are labeling their drawings).

THE IMPORTANCE OF CLARITY

Clear criteria and specific instructions increase the chances that students will produce the desired work. Often, what seem like adequate instructions are not consistent with students' actual responses (especially if they are responding to open-ended questions). Our own reactions become, *"no, that is not what I asked for"* or we repeatedly write in their work, *"you did not explain how you arrived at this conclusion."* Sometimes prompts are too general, resulting in students' misunderstandings about what to discuss. Or, in other cases, we may fail to specify criteria, such as, *"explain what data are supporting your conclusion."* In other words, if you want students to explain how they arrived at a solution, say it clearly in the instructions. If they are allowed to respond in nonwriting mode (e.g., with drawings), that needs to be specified. Having clear criteria can also help to provide feedback that is helpful for students to improve their learning. When the learning goals and the criteria do not match or they are not clear, "students often experience feedback as evaluation or grading rather than information for improvement" (Brookhart, 2012, p. 26).

Analyzing and Interpreting Evidence of Student Learning

Kroog et al. (2016) found that in about 72% of the artifacts collected, teachers' analyses focused mainly on whether the students' responses were correct or incorrect. This finding shows how challenging it is for teaches to analyze and interpret students' responses relative to the learning goals that focus on the disciplinary concepts, representations, procedures, and practices that they want their students to learn. If teachers are not clear on what they are looking for, the analysis and the interpretation of students' responses will be unfocused and, therefore, less productive for identifying what students need or what the teachers should reflect on. In order to provide appropriate feedback, you need to be able to analyze and interpret students' responses accurately, based on the criteria you shared with your students, and with an interpretative state of mind.

If your tasks are well thought out, analyzing and interpreting the student evidence becomes easier and more focused. Thus, your feedback also can be more focused, helpful, and appropriate. For example, if tasks are designed to reveal students' faulty reasoning, based on their errors, then it becomes easier to determine which students are making which types of errors. By analyzing the different types of errors, you can better determine what to do next. Are students' errors random or systematic? Is it possible to infer, based on these errors, the type of strategies students used to approach the task? If so, you can write more specific, individualized comments to each student or define a focused instructional move (e.g., discussing the steps for approaching the particular problem at hand).

Students' strengths and weaknesses are more easily recognized if you pay attention to the strategies students are using. Such *advance preparation* can help teachers to readily monitor the students' responses as they walk around the classroom. This strategy makes monitoring more efficient and helps teachers to proactively look for opportunities to provide feedback, individually (or in pairs and small groups) and, when appropriate, to the whole class. Furthermore, keeping students' strategies in mind helps teachers know on whom to call during classroom discussion and in which order (e.g., students with different strategies to solve that can provoke a good discussion; Smith & Stein, 2011)

On-the-fly formative assessment (or IFA) requires quick, often instant decisions about how to help students. If you have the schema of anticipated students' responses, IFA will be a more productive process. Similarly, when looking at students' written responses, if you have an interpretative state of mind, it will be easier to discern the disciplinary ideas in the responses.

Acting on Evidence of Student Learning

The most challenging formative assessment activity for teachers is to act on the information gathered from their students (Heritage, Kim, Vendlinski, & Herman, 2009; Ruiz-Primo & Furtak, 2006, 2007; Ruiz-Primo & Li, 2013; Schneider & Gowan, 2013). We have mentioned the study in which 58 teachers were observed on two occasions to capture information about their informal formative assessment practices in whole-class instructional mode. In that study, Ruiz-Primo and Kroog (2017) found that in 8% of the mathematics profiles and in 10% of the science profiles identified, teachers did not take any action based on the information collected. Even if they did, the actions were not of high quality. For example, they provide comments that were helpful, but general (e.g., read carefully). In this study, when the focus was formal formative assessment, what these researchers typically observed were teachers who *did not* look over the students' work before "discussing" assignments (e.g., a homework assignment). These teachers asked students to self-correct their assignments as they (the teacher) provided the correct responses to each question. In the best scenario, they occasionally asked students to provide the answer to a question. These teachers never knew which students had correct or incorrect responses, who truly understood, or what they understood. Yet, they moved to the next topic anyway.

Thinking About Acting Strategies

The analysis of the video collected for the DEMFAP project (Ruiz-Primo & Sands, 2009) showed that one-on-one and whole-class discussions are the pivot point for helping students to move forward in their learning. Even when the focus is on formal formative assessments (e.g., a quiz), discussion of the results is critical. If the focus of a quiz or a test is only on grades, students miss the opportunity to improve their learning (see also Black, 2015). Effective teachers do not miss the opportunity to turn a quiz into a feedback episode. Effective teachers *did* look over the students' work products before giving back the work to the students. Importantly, they discussed the work as students looked at what was just returned to them. During this discussion teachers (a) explained how the products were reviewed (in some cases, graded), (b) discussed how the class did overall, and (c) asked students to participate in the process. All these things happened in such a seamless manner, with such efficiency, that students were fully engaged in discussing how they did on the assignment. These teachers tended to wrap up the discussion with a take-away message (e.g., specific content areas where students were not doing well overall and that they needed to improve) and/or the implications for what would be coming as a result (e.g., changing the sequence of topics to teach).

We acknowledge that it is difficult for teachers to have the time to look over every student's work. Yet, there are times when it is important do this. Only when we have evidence from all students in the class can we have a sense of the students' strengths and weaknesses. That is, you have to pick those assignments (including quizzes or tests) that are important for you to know where *all* the students are at critical junctures of the unit you are teaching.

Ruiz-Primo, Sands, and Kroog (2016) observed practices of diverse quality when teachers did not have the opportunity to look at students' work. The worst scenario was already mentioned: teachers only provide the correct response and move to the next question or item of the assignment. Others, more effective teachers, ask students to work on correcting each other's assignment and discuss as a whole class the critical problems they have. Another strategy is one in which teachers select the questions to discuss with the whole class: either they pick two or three questions that are important for the topic at hand or they ask students to pick a question they (the students) consider was difficult to respond in the assignment. Effective teachers engage students in the discussion by asking them to model an approach, or asking why one strategy is better than another one. They focus on the errors students have, try to understand the students' rationale, and involve them in understanding a new approach.

When effective teachers have the opportunity to look over all the students' work, they describe how the class performed overall. They point to the successes and the missed questions. Sometimes this explanation is in the form of what was named (Ruiz-Primo & Kroog, 2015) thematic analysis (e.g., we are understanding "X", but we are still struggling with "Y"). Sometimes they provide exemplars of responses (positive or negative) explaining their characteristics. Other times, based on the information gained from what teachers observed in their analysis of the products, they start the acting by organizing students in groups in a purposeful manner (e.g., those students who understand something better and can explain it to others). Then the whole class comes together for a discussion that has a "take-away" message that in some cases is constructed with the students' help (e.g., the teacher asks, "so what are the three steps we need to follow? John, step 1. . . Lucy, step 2. . . Amhed, step 3. . . ") and in some others come from the teacher (e.g., "There are three steps we need to remember: First, . . . Second, . . . Third . . ."). How these discussions are wrapped up is an important characteristic that has been associated with higher student scores (Ruiz-Primo et al., 2013).

It is clear that the difficulty of acting upon the information collected can be mitigated if we practice the "anticipating" strategy discussed earlier because it helps to proactively think about strategies that can be used to respond to students, whether comments or instructional moves.

Closing Comments

In this chapter, we described the different challenges involved in implementing effective formative feedback practices, and some on the conditions that may affect the effectiveness with which feedback is implemented. We organized the challenges around the four formative assessment activities and using the formal and informal formative assessment practices as contexts. The challenges were discussed using empirical evidence from diverse studies. We provided some strategies to help improve the challenges and we highlighted the importance of your role in designing or selecting instructional tasks with certain characteristics that can help make students' thinking explicit and thus will help you to provide appropriate feedback.

References

Alexander, R. (2008). *Essays on pedagogy*. New York, NY: Routledge.

Bennett, N., Desforges, C., Cockburn, A., & Wilkinson, B. (1984). *The quality of pupil learning experiences*. London, UK: Lawrence Erlbaum.

Black, P. (2015). Formative assessment—an optimistic but incomplete vision. *Assessment in Education: Principles, Policy & Practice, 22*(1), 161–177.

Black, P., Wilson, M., & Yao, S-Y. (2011). Road maps for learning: A guide to the navigation of learning progressions. *Measurement: Interdisciplinary Research and Perspectives, 9*(2–3), 71–123.

Briggs, D., Alonzo, A., Schwab, C., & Wilson, M. (2006). Diagnostic assessment with ordered multiple-choice items. *Educational Assessment, 11*(1), 33–63.

Brookhart, S. (2012). Preventing feedback fizzle. *Educational Leadership, 70*(1), 25–29.

Cartier, J. L., Smith, M. S., Stein, M. S., & Ross, D. K. (2013). *Five practices for orchestrating productive task-based discussions in science*. Reston, VA: National Council of Teachers of Mathematics.

Colvin, G. (2008). *Talent is overrated: What really separates world-class performers from everybody else*. London, UK: Nicholas Brealey Publishing.

Davis, B. (1997). Listening for differences: An evolving conception of mathematics teaching. *Journal for Research in Mathematics Education, 28*(3), 355–376.

Doyle, W. (1983). Academic work. *Review of Educational Research, 53*, 159–199.

Ericsson, K. A. (1996). The acquisition of expert performance: An introduction to some issues. In K. A. Ericsson (Ed.), *The road to excellence: The acquisition of expert performance in the arts and science, sports, and games* (pp. 14–64). New York, NY: Lawrence Erlbaum.

Ericsson, K. A., Krampe, R. T., & Tesch-Römer, C. (1993). The role of deliberate practice in the acquisition of expert performance. *Psychological Review, 100*(3), 363–406.

Hattie, J., Fisher, D., & Frey, N. (2016). Do they hear you? *Educational Leadership, 73*(7), 16–21.

Heritage, M. (2013). *Formative assessment in practice: A process of inquiry and action.* Cambridge, MA: Harvard Education Press.

Heritage, M., Kim, J., Vendlinski, T., & Herman, J. (2009). From evidence to action: A seamless process in formative assessment? *Educational Measurement: Issues and Practice, 28*(3), 24–31.

Hiebert, J., & Grouws, D. A. (2007). The effects of classroom mathematics teaching on students' learning. In J. F. K. Lester (Ed.), *Second handbook of research on mathematics teaching and learning* (pp. 371–404). Charlotte: Information Age Publishing.

Jacobs, V., Lamb, L., & Philipp, R. (2010). Professional noticing of children's mathematical thinking. *Journal for Research in Mathematics Education, 41*(2), 169–202.

Jordan, B., & Putz, P. (2004). Assessment as practice: Notes on measures, tests, and targets. *Human Organization, 63,* 346–358.

Kennewell, S. (2001). Using affordance and constraints to evaluate the use of information and communications technology in teaching and learning. *Journal of Information Technology for Teacher Education, 10*(1–2), 101–116.

Kroog, H., King Hess, K., & Ruiz-Primo, M. A. (2016). Implement effective and efficient approaches to formal formative assessment that will save time and boost student learning. *Educational Leadership, 73*(7), 22–25.

Marshall, B., Carmichael, P., & Drummond, M-J. (2007). Learning how to learn in classrooms. In M. James, R. McCormick, P. Black, P. Carmichael, M-J. Drummond, A. Fox, J. MacBeath, B. Marshall, D. Pedder, R. Procter, S. Swaffield, J. Swann, & D. Wiliam (Eds.), *Improving learning how to learn: Classrooms, schools, and network* (pp. 56–71). New York, NY: Routledge.

Nebelsick-Gullett, L., Hamen Farrar, C., Huff, K., & Packman, S. (2013). Design of interim assessment for instructional purpose: A case study using evidence centered design in advanced placement. In R. W. Lissitz (Ed.), *Informing the practice of teaching using formative and interim assessments* (pp. 21–48). Charlotte, NC: Information Age Publishing, Inc.

O'Brian, J. (2013). *Formative feedback in context.* Doctoral dissertation. Denver, CO: University of Colorado Denver.

Perrenoud, P. (1998). From formative evaluation to a controlled regulation of learning process. Towards a wider conceptual field. *Assessment in Education: Principles, Policy, & Practice, 5*(1), 85–102.

Ruiz-Primo, M. A. (2010). *Developing and Evaluating Measures of Formative Assessment Practice (DEMFAP) theoretical and methodological approach.* Internal manuscript. University of Colorado Denver. Denver, CO: Laboratory of Educational Assessment, Research, and InnovatioN (LEARN).

Ruiz-Primo, M. A., & Furtak, E. M. (2006). Informal formative assessment and scientific inquiry: Exploring teachers' practices and student learning. *Educational Assessment, 11*(3–4), 205–235.

Ruiz-Primo, M. A., & Furtak, E. M. (2007). Exploring teachers' informal formative assessment practices and students' understanding in the context of scientific inquiry. *Journal of Research in Science Teaching, 44*(1), 57–84.

Ruiz-Primo, M. A., Iverson, H., & Sands, D. (2013). *Video logging approach.* Document for Second Advisory Board Meeting. Laboratory of Educational Assessment, Research, and Innovation. Denver, CO: University of Colorado Denver.

Ruiz-Primo, M. A., & Kroog, H. (2015). *A suite of instruments to measure formative assessment practices in the classroom.* Denver, CO: University of Colorado Denver. Laboratory of Educational Assessment, Research, and Innovation.

Ruiz-Primo, M. A., & Kroog, H. (2016). *The impact of observation sampling strategies on the accuracy of inferences about teachers' formative assessment practices.* Paper submitted for publication.

Ruiz-Primo, M. A., & Kroog, H. (2017, April). *Variations of formative assessment practices across instructional tasks.* Paper presented at the AERA annual meeting, San Antonio, TX.

Ruiz-Primo, M. A., Kroog, H., & Sands, D. I. (2015, August). *Teachers' judgments on-the-fly: Teachers' response patterns in the context of informal formative assessment.* Paper presented at the EARLI Biennial Conference, Limassol, Cyprus.

Ruiz-Primo, M. A., & Li, M. (2013). Analyzing teachers' feedback practices in response to students' work in science classrooms. Special Issue on Using Evidence to Take Action: Strategies Teachers Use to Deconstruct Student Work. *Applied Measurement in Education, 26*(3), 163–175.

Ruiz-Primo, M. A., & Sands, D. (2009). *Developing and Evaluating Measures of Formative Assessment Practices (DEMFAP),* Institute of Education Sciences. Cognition and Student Learning. Award ID: R305A100571.

Ruiz-Primo, M. A., Sands, D., & Kroog, H. (2016). *Developing and evaluating measures of Formative Assessment Practices (DEMFAP): Technical report on instrument development and evaluation.* Technical report submitted to the Institute of Education Sciences. IES Grant # R305A100571. Washington, DC.

Schneider, M. C., & Gowan, P. (2013). Investigating teachers' skills in interpreting evidence of student learning. *Applied Measurement in Education, 26*, 191–204. doi:10.1080/08957347.2013.793185

Smith, M. S., & Stein, M. K. (2011). *Five practices for orchestrating productive mathematics discussions.* Reston, VA: National Council of Teachers of Mathematics.

Stein, M. K., Engle, R. A., Smith, M. S., & Hughes, E. K. (2008). Orchestrating productive mathematical discussions: Five practices for helping teachers move beyond show and tell. *Mathematical Thinking and Learning, 10*(4), 313–340.

Stein, M. K., Grover, B. W., & Henningsen, M. (1996). Building student capacity for mathematical thinking and reasoning: An analysis of mathematical tasks used in reform classrooms. *American Educational Research Journal, 33*(2), 455–488.

Stobart, G. (2014). *The expert learner: Challenging the myth of ability.* Berkshire, UK: Open University Press.

Syed, M. (2010). *Bounce: Mozart, Federer, Picasso, Beckman, and the science of success.* New York, NY: Harper.

Sztajn, P., Confrey, J., Wilson, P. H., & Edgington, C. (2012). Learning trajectory based instruction: Toward a theory of teaching. *Educational Researcher, 41*(5), 147–156. doi:10.3102/0013189X12442801

Threlfall, J. (2005). The formative use of assessment information in planning—the notion of contingent planning. *British Journal of Educational Studies, 53*(1), 54–65.

Torrance, H., & Pryor, J. (2001). Developing formative assessment in the classroom: Using action to explore and modify theory. *British Educational Research Journal, 27*(5), 615–631.

White, M. A. (1971). The view from the student's desk. In M. L. Silberman (Ed.), *The experience of schooling* (pp. 337–345). New York: Holt, Rinehart and Winston.

5

Feedback Here, There, and Everywhere

Most of this book has been about feedback from teachers to students. That is the most common kind of feedback, and the feedback that students often value the most (Gamlem & Smith, 2013). However, feedback comes from many other sources, as well. In this chapter, we discuss feedback from other sources: feedback from the learners themselves (self-assessment), feedback from peers, and feedback from computers.

All sources of feedback can be important parts of the regulation of learning if done effectively. Self-assessment can and should be part of the self-regulation of learning (Zimmerman & Schunk, 2011). Like teacher feedback, feedback from peers, computers, and other resources is part of the information from other sources (Allal, 2011) in the co-regulation of learning. But they are not interchangeable. Each source of feedback functions somewhat differently, and with somewhat different perceptions by students and effects on learning.

Self-Assessment

Developing assessment-capable learners is the ultimate goal of learning, instruction, and feedback (Brown & Harris, 2014). Many teachers show an intuitive understanding of this fact when they lament to students, "What are you going to do when I'm not here anymore?" Equipping learners to be assessment-capable has taken on new importance as learning theorists have realized that students construct their own meaning. Phrases like "lifelong learning" and "learning how to learn" have become common in schools.

Accuracy of Self-Assessment Judgments

Several reviews of the self-assessment literature (Andrade & Brown, 2016; Andrade & Valtcheva, 2009; Brown & Harris, 2013; Falchikov & Boud, 1989; Ross, 2006) have been published in recent years. Regarding the accuracy of student self-assessment judgments, research reviews show that students who are better at self-assessment are more likely to be modest in their assessments of their own work. High achievers tend to assess their work lower, and low achievers tend to assess their work higher, than their teachers do. Most students can accurately evaluate how well they scored on tests. Factors that contribute to more accurate, competent self-assessment include training and practice in self-assessment, opportunities to discuss criteria, the nature of the task and criteria (simple and concrete tasks work best), experience with the subject, age, and ability.

While students are generally accurate in their self-assessment (Falchikov & Boud, 1989), studies that examine the accuracy of self-grading miss the more important point of self-assessment as currently practiced. As the formative assessment framework in Chapter 1 shows, the benefits of self-assessment for generating formative feedback information, student motivation, and improvement of learning lie in using self-assessment *during* the formative learning cycle. During the learning cycle, there is still time for students to revise their work, do more study to clarify fuzzy points, and in general figure out "Where am I?" in relation to my learning goal and "How do I get there?" Self-assessment episodes that help students regulate their learning and improve can be effective feedback episodes.

Self-Assessment and the Regulation of Learning

As cognitive learning theories became more widely accepted, and formative assessment has come to be seen as a practice congruent with the notion that students make their own meaning when they learn, researchers have studied the importance of student self-assessment as part of the regulation of learning. Considered in this way, student self-assessment (and self-feedback) is both an instructional and an assessment strategy. Self-assessment helps students monitor where they are in relation to their learning goals, and helps them plan where they will go next (Ross, 2006; Brown & Harris, 2013). Brown and Harris (2013) found that self-assessment enhances an internal locus of control, supports self-referenced judgments over norm-referenced judgments, and leads to improved self-efficacy, engagement, behavior, and student-teacher relationships. Self-assessment can increase both achievement (learning) and learner autonomy, creating more self-regulated learners (Andrade & Valtcheva, 2009).

A critical component of self-assessment is having clear criteria, communicated to students so they can understand and use them. Self-assessment helps students connect at a deep level with their learning goals and criteria for success. Recall the studies in Chapter 2, about the necessity of students holding clear goals for learning. In those studies, the way that students developed clear goals was to develop or use rubrics that communicated the criteria for good work. However, other ways of communicating criteria are possible, as well (Panadero, Tapia, & Huertas, 2012). It is only when students can apply criteria to the work they have done that they know how they are doing and whether they are, in fact, learning. These studies have been conducted in all grade levels, from primary to tertiary education, and in many different subject areas (Brookhart & Chen, 2015).

Several reviews of the self-assessment literature have shown how self-assessment can help K–12 students develop positive attitudes toward learning and their ability to regulate their own learning.

Andrade and Valtcheva (2009) found students' positive attitudes toward self-assessment in a specific course did not transfer to other courses. A probable explanation is that in self-assessment, understanding specific criteria is what is important. To the extent that criteria in other courses were different, positive attitudes based on a feeling of understanding of criteria would not transfer. Andrade and Valtcheva (2009) also found that positive attitudes toward self-assessment stemmed from the formative nature of the experience; students' attitudes toward self-assessment were negative if the self-assessment was used for grading (i.e., summative assessment).

Brown and Harris (2013) investigated self-assessment in K–12 education by reviewing 84 studies under five research questions. Their first question asked about the relationship between self-assessment and student academic achievement. They found the median effect size for using self-assessment was 0.40 to 0.45, a moderate impact, although some studies reported no effect or very small effects. Training students in self-assessment, using models of effective answers, teacher feedback, clear criteria, and predicting future performance were all associated with learning gains from student self-assessment. Brown and Harris concluded (p. 383), "It is the implementation and complexity of the self-assessment, more so than the type, which generates the positive effects."

Their second research question was about the effects of self-assessment on the self-regulation of learning. They found some studies that reported improved motivation, self-efficacy, engagement, behavior, and quality of student-teacher relationships as a result of self-assessment, although there is not a solid research base in this area yet. Their third research question was about student perceptions of self-assessment. There was mixed evidence here. Some students enjoyed self-assessment, although sometimes they found it boring or were concerned about having their self-assessments made public to other students, parents, or teachers.

Brown and Harris's (2013) fourth research question was about accuracy of student self-assessment. Higher-performing students usually evaluated their work more accurately than lower-performing students. In addition, elementary students were more optimistic in their self-assessments and more likely to use effort and superficial features of their work in their self-assessments.

The fifth question was about the relationship of self-assessment accuracy to assessment tasks. In general, more specific tasks with specific criteria were assessed more accurately. Their overall conclusion was that self-assessment can contribute to improved learning and self-regulation, but only if the self-assessment involves deep engagement with the process of self-regulation and therefore, we would argue, with the formative learning cycle described in Chapter 1. Brown and Harris (2013, p. 370) observed that

> lack of competence in a domain (as would be expected in a low progress learner or a beginner) has a dual-handicapping effect; such people are not very good in the domain and, at the same time, are not aware that they are not good in the domain.

Incorporating self-assessment into classroom practice can be difficult. Wylie and Lyon (2015) studied mathematics and science teachers who participated in a two-year, school-based professional development program in formative assessment called Keeping Learning on Track. There was not much change over the two years in teachers' use of self-assessment or peer assessment. Teachers used peer assessment slightly more than they used self-assessment, although most of the peer assessment was closer to collaborative learning than to assessment.

Because self-assessment holds such an important place in the formative learning cycle and provides an internal source of feedback—the only feedback mechanism to do so—we argue that students should be taught to use high-quality self-assessment practices and given regular and routine opportunities to do so during their learning. The self-assessment literature, and the feedback literature cited previously in this book, together, supports the following recommendations for self-assessment practice:

- Make the criteria by which students will assess their work clear and understandable to students.
- Design tools (e.g., rubrics, checklists, or sets of guiding questions) that help students use the criteria, and give students instruction and practice in their use.

- Give students training and practice in self-assessment, and give them feedback on the quality of their self-assessments. Teach self-assessment as a core curricular competence that helps students self-regulate and improve their learning (Brown & Harris, 2014).
- In your own feedback, use language that helps students connect the quality of their self-assessment with the effectiveness of their next steps in learning.
- Use self-assessment for formative rather than summative purposes (Andrade & Valtcheva, 2009).

Peer Assessment

Peer assessment differs from self-assessment in several important ways. As pointed out above, self-assessment yields feedback that is internal to the student. Andrade (2010) maintains that students have exclusive access to their thoughts and may be considered "the definitive source of formative assessment" (p. 90). Students' assessment and critique of their own work can yield plans for next steps in learning and improvement of work. In contrast, peer feedback is an external source of regulation for a learner, similar to teacher feedback but from a less authoritative source.

Peer feedback yields suggestions for improvement that must be evaluated again, for quality and relevance, before applying these suggestions to their work. That is, the student will evaluate the source of peer feedback—and should, just as we teach students to judge the credibility of any source—as well as the usefulness of the feedback for improving the work. Contrast this with teacher feedback, which, while also an external source of regulation, comes from an authoritative source. For students providing feedback to others, peer assessment functions as an instructional activity for them, providing more familiarity with the criteria and an example of work to analyze. The exercise of providing peer feedback may yield a better understanding of the qualities of good work, but this understanding must be applied to their own work before improvement is possible. In both cases, for both peer assessor and assessee, the formative information is indirect.

We found two reviews of peer assessment in K–12 education (Panadero, 2016; Topping, 2013) and one review of both peer and self-assessment (Sebba, Deakin Crick, Yu, Lawson, Harlen, & Durant, 2008). Panadero (2016) found that early research on peer assessment was mostly concerned with the reliability and validity of summative scores. His reading of more recent peer assessment literature is that peer assessment now is conceptualized more as a collaborative learning activity than a source of assessment information. His review found that psychological safety and trust, important elements of peer assessment, are not easy to build into the process. Students may perceive peer assessment as unfair because the assessors—their peers—are not the knowledgeable evaluators they perceive their teachers to be. He found there is a friendship bias in peer assessment, with peers assessing friends' work more highly.

Topping (2013) used Piagetian and Vygotskian perspectives in a model of peer assessment. He recognized the important roles of emotion, motivation, and communication, as well as cognition, in peer assessment. He found the research base for peer assessment as a support of learning to be weak in K–12 settings. Little evidence suggested peer assessment supported learning at the elementary level, although there was some evidence at the secondary level. However, secondary students questioned the value of peer assessment and noted that the feedback from peer assessment may not be accurate, a similar theme to the higher education literature. Affirming and suggestive peer feedback had generally positive effects on learning, but didactic and corrective feedback had generally negative effects.

Sebba et al. (2008) reviewed studies of the impact of self- and peer assessment on students in secondary schools published from 1985 to 2005. Fifteen of 26 reviewed studies reported on performance or achievement outcomes, and nine of those reported an increase. Nine of these studies measured student self-esteem, of which seven showed a positive effect for self- and/or peer assessment. Seventeen out of 20 studies showed a positive effect of self- and/or peer assessment for student engagement with learning, for example, setting goals, and for taking personal responsibility for learning. The effects of self- and peer assessment were related to the existence of a classroom culture where students were allowed and encouraged to be independent learners, and where teachers adjusted their teaching in response to student feedback.

Although the impacts of self-assessment on learning seem greater than for peer assessment, at least one study comparing the two has found no difference in their effects. Meusen-Beekman, Joosten-ten Brinke, and Boshuizen (2014) studied the relationship between self-regulated learning and peer or self-assessment with sixth-grade students in the Netherlands. Students used either peer or self-assessment of three writing assignments, and a comparison group did not. They also co-created the criteria for their writing tasks, set goals, made plans, and used checklists to monitor their progress. In these ways, the students provided themselves and each other with both task- and process-level feedback during all of the phases of self-regulation of learning. Self- and peer assessment was positively associated with self-regulation and intrinsic motivation, although there were no differences between the peer and self-assessment conditions. It appears that in this case the deep focus on criteria and on the process of self-regulation was more important than whether the feedback came from oneself or a peer.

Despite the difficulties and risks, both Panadero (2016) and Topping (2013) recommended that peer assessment be pursued as a collaborative learning activity more than as a source of feedback. We concur, and we emphasize that peer assessment should yield learning benefits for both the peer assessor and assessee. When done well, peer assessment can foster a deeper understanding of the learning goal that is so important to formative assessment ("Where am I going?") as well as to the self-regulation of learning more generally (Pintrich & Zusho, 2002; Zimmerman & Schunk, 2011) because students must work deeply with criteria and with an example of student work. Working with criteria and examining student work are known to clarify a student's understanding of learning goals (Andrade & Brookhart, 2014; Heritage, 2010; Wiliam, 2011).

The peer assessment literature, and the feedback literature cited previously in this book, support recommendations for peer assessment practice. Many of these are very similar to the recommendations for self-assessment:

- Make the criteria by which students will assess their work clear and understandable to students.
- Design tools (e.g., rubrics, checklists, or sets of guiding questions) that help students use the criteria, and give students instruction and practice in their use.
- Give students training and practice in peer assessment, and give them feedback on the quality of their peer assessments.
- Use peer assessment for formative rather than summative purposes.
- Use peer assessment as a collaborative learning activity rather than a definitive source of feedback for revision of work.

Technology as a Source of Feedback

Increasingly, technology provides a delivery mechanism for feedback on students' work. Students experience feedback from technology in at least two ways. Technology can be simply the delivery mechanism, as when teachers use digital programs to give feedback on student work that is submitted electronically. For example, if a student submits a word-processed essay, the teacher can use the 'comments' function to supply written feedback. Or, technology can be both the delivery mechanism and the source of the feedback. In computer-based instruction, the computer program "gives" the feedback. Of course, decisions about the nature of the feedback and the comments, if any, have been planned by human designers.

Human Feedback Delivered Electronically

Teachers can deliver feedback electronically, either in writing or through audio or video files, using the same principles for effective feedback described in Chapter 3. When work is submitted in word processing files, teachers can use the 'comments' function for this purpose. Written feedback can also be provided via e-mail. The same feedback principles that apply in face-to-face classrooms apply for feedback given by instructors in online learning (Chetwynd & Dobbyn, 2011). Descriptive feedback without grades attached followed by opportunities for students to use the feedback is particularly important for online courses, where it is tempting to provide feedback on required assignments at the same time they are graded. Providing feedback that not only retrospectively critiques a particular assignment, but also gives suggestions for improvement (Chetwynd and Dobbyn (p. 68) called this "future-altering" feedback), is also an issue in online learning, just as for face-to-face learning.

One of the authors routinely gives feedback to students via computer. Some of this feedback is to teacher education students taking online courses, where assignments are submitted as word processing files. Some of this feedback has been to teachers participating in a professional development program, where the assignments were scanned collections of student work and teacher reflections. In both cases, feedback via e-mail worked well. In addition to following all the principles for effective feedback, choosing words carefully and giving students opportunities for revision, it was particularly important to check the feedback for tone. The disembodied words in an e-mail communication can more easily be taken as criticism or evaluation, rather than description, if the author of the feedback is not especially careful about the message.

AbuSeileek (2013) studied computer-mediated (via word processor) peer feedback in an English as a Foreign Language class at a university in Jordan. The students were trying to learn to correct 11 major error types in their English essay writing: capitalization, fragments and run-ons, misused words, and so on. Sixty-four students were randomly assigned to four groups. One group only used the track changes function to give and receive peer feedback. The second group only used the word processor's built-in corrective feedback (e.g., the word processors' automatic identification of misspelled words or grammar errors). The third group used both kinds of computer-mediated feedback. A fourth group neither gave nor received any corrective feedback on their writing. These groups all proceeded with instruction in English, in class, with the exception of how they got feedback on their short essay assignments. The group using both track changes and the word processor for feedback outscored the other groups. All of the feedback groups outscored the control group on the test of English usage. In this design, the use of track changes also involved the use of peer feedback.

With the advent of video recording functions in phones, cameras, and webcams, some teachers are beginning to experiment with video feedback. Another way to give video feedback is to use screen capturing software so the student views the teacher reading and talking about the work (e.g., www.youtube.com/watch?v=YS4v02kHttA). This feedback can also be shared within an online course or via e-mail or posting.

Feedback in Computer-Based Instruction

Feedback in computer-based instruction comes from the computer program itself. But it is human designers and instructors who specify the nature of the feedback. Traditional feedback research has been used to inform the decisions made in designing feedback for instructional software (Mory, 2004). More recently, research has been done directly on the effects of various kinds of feedback from computer-based instruction. Most computer-based instruction provides knowledge of results—feedback on the correctness of answers. Some computer-based instruction also provides elaborated feedback—descriptions of the qualities of the work. Mason and Bruning (2001) categorized eight different types of computer-provided feedback that have been studied.

- *No feedback*—typically used as a control condition (e.g., a total quiz score with no information about individual items)
- *Knowledge-of-response*—computer provides item-level correct/incorrect information
- *Answer-until-correct*—learner must stay on the same test item until it is correct
- *Knowledge-of-correct-response*—computer provides item-level correct/incorrect information and gives the correct answer
- *Topic-contingent*—computer provides item-level correct/incorrect information and routs the student back to learning material or to additional material

- *Response-contingent*—computer provides item-level correct/incorrect information and an explanation of why the incorrect answer is wrong and the correct answer is right
- *Bug-related*—computer provides item-level correct/incorrect information and information about specific errors (obtained from a "bug library" of common errors)
- *Attribute-isolation*—computer provides item-level correct/incorrect information and highlights important attributes of the concept being learned

You will notice that one of the cardinal principles for crafting effective feedback—making one or more suggestions for next steps—is absent in all of these types. Some of the types of feedback Mason and Bruning described, however, contain enough information that students can figure out what might be a useful next step, for example, item-level correct/incorrect information could be used to focus future studying.

Mason and Bruning (2001) reported mixed findings about elaborative feedback in computer-based instruction. Some studies found elaborative feedback more effective than knowledge of results alone and some have not (Mason & Bruning, 2001). The effectiveness of elaborative feedback in computer-based instruction seems to depend on both the student and the task. On average, lower-ability students have been found to benefit more from immediate, specific feedback (e.g., answer correct/incorrect) and higher-ability students have been found to benefit more from feedback that requires them to more actively process information (e.g., links to resources). However, in general the trend is for more elaborative feedback to be more effective for learning. This is consistent with the findings for feedback generally, where specific description is better for learning than general feedback.

A more recent meta-analysis of studies of feedback in computer-based learning environments reached similar conclusions (Van der Kleij, Feskens, and Eggen, 2015) (meta-analysis is a quantitative synthesis of research results that shows overall trends). Van der Kleij and her colleagues computed 70 different effect sizes from 40 different studies. All students in both experimental and control groups received item-based feedback, that is, feedback after each item in a test, and then took a post-test based on the same content. Type of feedback was coded according to whether there was no feedback, knowledge of results (right/wrong), providing the correct answer, or elaborated feedback (providing an explanation). Elaborated feedback resulted in the largest effect size (0.49, representing a half standard deviation difference between the experimental and control groups). However, even knowledge of results (0.05) and providing the correct answer (0.32) were more effective than no feedback. The effect of elaborated feedback was especially large if the learning outcomes measured were higher-order learning, as much as 0.77 if the control condition was no feedback, and 0.69 if the control condition was knowledge of results. Effect sizes were larger in mathematics than in social sciences, science, or language.

Finally, interest is growing in electronic game-based learning and what is sometimes called "gamification" in education. Game-based learning is the name given to the movement to use educational video games as learning tools (McClarty, Orr, Frey, Dolan, Vassilleve, & McVay, 2012). Game-based learning differs from regular computer-based instruction in that the learning takes place within the context of a game; this contrasts with other computer-based instructional programs in the form of computer-based lessons, modules, or tutorials. Gamification is a broader term than game-based learning (Surendeleg, Murwa, Yun, & Kim, 2014) and includes using game design elements in the learning environment (Caponetto, Earp, & Ott, 2014). Games are based on learning principles that include the use of play, opportunities for continued practice, clear goals, and immediate feedback, and the opportunity to personalize learning (McClarty et al., 2012). Connelly, Boyle, MacArthur, Hainey, and Boyle (2012) reviewed empirical evidence of the outcomes and impacts of using computer games in education. They found the two most frequent outcomes were motivational outcomes and content knowledge acquisition. Other intended outcomes for various educational computer games included perceptual and cognitive skills, behavior change, physiological outcomes, and social outcomes. They located only 17 studies with good-quality research designs that investigated the effects of games on knowledge acquisition and content understanding. The evidence in these 17 studies was mixed regarding whether game-based learning increases knowledge and content understanding.

For purposes of this book, our interest in game-based learning and gamification is based on the opportunities they present for immediate, personalized feedback. This literature is just in its beginning stages, and as far as we are aware no research has separated out the effects of feedback from the effects of the other aspects of game-based learning. This is not the case, however, for intelligent tutoring systems, where the effects of feedback have been isolated and studied. We turn next to this form of computer-based instruction.

Intelligent Tutoring Systems

Intelligent Tutoring Systems (ITS) are different from computer-assisted instruction and computer-based training because they have an "intelligent" feature that interprets student responses in terms of student learning before selecting the next task—rather than just giving a harder or easier task—and provides feedback to students along the way. Ma, Adesope, Nesbit, and Liu (2014, p. 902) describe an ITS as a computer system that performs the following for each student:

1. Completes tutoring functions by (a) presenting information, (b) asking questions or assigning learning tasks, (c) providing feedback or hints, (d) answering student questions, or (e) offering prompts to provoke cognitive, motivational or meta-cognitive change.
2. Constructs a model of effective learning in the domain, and then from student responses either constructs a model of student's understanding or motivation or locates the student's current understanding in the multidimensional domain model.
3. Uses the student model (#2) to adapt one or more of the tutoring functions (#1).

ITS are designed to provide students with a formative assessment experience. In fact, the ITS principles are remarkably similar to the formative assessment cycle described in Chapter 1. ITS include attention to deep understanding of the goal of learning (ITS use a domain model, not just an inventory of easier to harder tasks), providing feedback (comments, hints, knowledge of results, explanation of results, depending on the ITS), using student work as evidence of student thinking, not just correctness (constructing a student model), and then targeting next instructional moves (selecting learning tasks based on the model of student thinking). In particular, the ability to focus on student thinking every time student evidence is reviewed, and use student thinking as the basis on which to provide both comments and next instructional moves, makes ITS remarkable in light of the learning and assessment theories we have reviewed in prior chapters.

A recent meta-analysis of ITS shows that using ITS for instruction is associated with higher achievement outcomes than any other instructional method tested, except for human tutoring (Ma et al., 2014). Ma et al. summarized 107 effect sizes and found using ITS was associated with a 0.42 standard deviation increase in achievement over teacher-led large group instruction, a 0.57 increase over other kinds of computer-based instruction, and a 0.35 increase over textbook- or workbook-driven instruction. ITS were associated with less achievement ($g = -0.11$) than individual human tutoring and with similar achievement ($g = 0.05$) to small-group instruction.

In ITS, providing "feedback" can come in the form of comments, providing hints to the right answer, or comments adjusted for the history of student responses, or it can come in the form of next instructional moves as the program selects the student's next exercise. Ma and colleagues (2014) tested whether the ITS in a study provided feedback comments or not, which turned out to make no difference. They observed (p. 914),

> It is notable that when we reread the studies in which the ITS did not provide response feedback we found that in each case the primary adaptive feature was individualized task selection, an observation that suggests individualized task selection may offer benefits comparable to the well-established, positive effects of feedback on learning.

This finding is an affirmation, albeit only in the context of computer-based instruction, that targeted instructional moves (in this case, individualized task selection based on students' prior response history) functions as a form of feedback that can be as effective as feedback in the form of comments. In this regard, the ITS literature supports a main theme of this book, that both comments and next instructional moves are types of feedback.

Student Responses to Feedback

As we have already stressed, feedback is only useful if students understand it and use it for improvement. Feedback cannot function as part of the formative learning cycle or as part of the self-regulation of learning unless it is used, and to be used it must first be interpreted. Most descriptions of formative feedback include an exhortation to design immediate, or at least near-term, opportunities for students to use feedback (e.g., Brookhart, 2017), as we have in Chapter 3.

Draper (2009) suggests there are at least six possible student interpretations of feedback (p. 308):

1. Technical knowledge or method (e.g., I did not use the best information or method to complete the task, either of which can be improved).
2. Effort (e.g., I did not leave enough time to do a task well).
3. Method of learning about a task (e.g., I realize I did not seek out the right information about the task, or did not understand the criteria for the task).
4. Ability (e.g., I just do not have the aptitude to succeed at a task).
5. Random (e.g., I did what I was supposed to, so success is possible next time without adjustment or revision).
6. The judgment process was wrong (e.g., I received incorrect feedback).

He argues that for feedback to foster improvement and learning, the feedback must help the learner do something differently. However, what a student would do differently depends on the way the student interprets the feedback. Typically, we hope for one of the first three interpretations and expect the student to adjust understanding (perhaps by seeking out new or additional information), skill (by increasing practice), or effort, or seek more information about the task and criteria. Students will only do that if they interpret the feedback as intended. If they interpret the feedback as random or incorrect, for example, they will not try to adjust their learning or their work. Finally, he points out that there is a seventh option: simple despair or giving up, or blaming someone else. As we have pointed out before, feedback should never foster student despair (Covington, 1992).

Some research has investigated what kinds of feedback students prefer and find most useful. Studies from Australia (Ferguson, 2011), New Zealand (Harris, Brown, & Harnett, 2014; Peterson & Irving, 2008), Norway (Gamlem & Smith, 2013), the United Kingdom (Murtagh, 2014; Pokorny & Pickford, 2010; Weaver, 2006), and the United States (Pajares & Graham, 1998), with student samples from middle school through college, are unanimous in the finding that students value feedback that helps them improve. They consider suggestions for improvement positive and express that feedback is only worthwhile if it is helpful for learning. In contrast, teachers sometimes feel that effective feedback is feedback which makes students feel good (Pajares & Graham, 1998) or just explains a grade. Please, help us "get the word out" that this is *not* what students want, and not what they consider helpful or useful. Most students crave information that helps them improve and see that as positive.

Closing Comments

In this chapter, we discussed feedback from student self-assessment and peer assessment and feedback from technology. A main theme has been that the characteristics of effective feedback remain the same as presented in Chapter 3, although they may be operationalized differently depending on the sources. Elaborated feedback, describing what was done well and what next steps to take, using criteria that students clearly understand, and delivered as part of a formative assessment cycle where there is opportunity for revision and further learning, is on balance the most effective.

We can counter Draper's student responses 4 through 6, and also the despair he observed for some students, with skillful use of the feedback methods described and advocated in Chapters 2 through 4. Chapter 6 concludes our book by considering how feedback may be improved.

References

AbuSeileek, A. F. (2013). Using track changes and word processor to provide corrective feedback to learners in writing. *Journal of Computer Assisted Learning*, 29, 319–333.

Allal, L. (2011). Pedagogy, didactics and the co-regulation of learning: A perspective from the French-language world of educational research. *Research Papers in Education*, 26(3), 329–336.

Andrade, H. L. (2010). Students as the definite source of formative assessment: Academic self-assessment and the self-regulation of learning. In H. L. Andrade & G. J. Cizek (Eds.), *Handbook of formative assessment* (pp. 90–105). New York, NY: Routledge. Taylor Francis Group.

Andrade, H. L., & Brookhart, S. M. (2014, April). *Assessment as the regulation of learning*. Paper presented at the annual meeting of the American Educational Research Association, Philadelphia, PA.

Andrade, H. L., & Brown, G. T. L. (2016). Student self-assessment in the classroom. In G. T. L. Brown & L. Harris (Eds.), *Human factors and social conditions of assessment* (pp. 319–334). London: Routledge.

Andrade, H. L., & Valtcheva, A. (2009). Promoting learning and achievement through self-assessment. *Theory into Practice*, 48, 12–19.

Brookhart, S. M. (2017). *How to give effective feedback to your students* (2nd ed.). Alexandria, VA: ASCD.

Brookhart, S. M., & Chen, F. (2015). The quality and effectiveness of descriptive rubrics. *Educational Review*, 67(3), 343–368.

Brown, G. T. L., & Harris, L. R. (2013). Student self-assessment. In. J. H. McMillan (Ed.), *Sage handbook of research on classroom assessment* (pp. 367–393). Los Angeles: Sage.

Brown, G. T. L., & Harris, L. R. (2014). The future of self-assessment in classroom practice: Reframing self-assessment as a core competency. *Frontline Learning Research*, 3, 22–30.

Caponetto, I., Earp, J., & Ott, M. (2014, October). *Gamification and education: A literature review.* Unpublished manuscript.

Chetwynd, F., & Dobbyn, C. (2011). Assessment, feedback and marking guides in distance education. *Open Learning: The Journal of Open, Distance and e-Learning, 26*(1), 67–78.

Connelly, T. M., Boyle, E. A., MacArthur, E., Hainey, T., & Boyle, J. M. (2012). A systematic literature review of empirical evidence on computer games and serious games. *Computers and Education, 59,* 661–686.

Covington, M. V. (1992). *Making the grade: A self-worth perspective on motivation and school reform.* Cambridge: Cambridge University Press.

Draper, S. (2009). What are learners actually regulating when given feedback? *British Journal of Educational Technology, 40*(2), 306–315.

Falchikov, N., & Boud, D. (1989). Student self-assessment in higher education: A meta-analysis. *Review of Educational Research, 59*(4), 395–430.

Ferguson, P. (2011). Student perceptions of quality feedback in teacher education. *Assessment and Evaluation in Higher Education, 36,* 51–62.

Gamlem, S. M., & Smith, K. (2013). Student perceptions of classroom feedback. *Assessment in Education: Principles, Policy and Practice, 20,* 150–169.

Harris, L. R., Brown, G. T. L., & Harnett, J. A. (2014). Understanding classroom feedback practices: A study of New Zealand student experiences, perceptions, and emotional responses. *Educational Assessment, Evaluation and Accountability, 26,* 107–133.

Heritage, M. (2010). *Formative assessment: Making it happen in the classroom.* Thousand Oaks, CA: Corwin.

Ma, W., Adesope, O. O., Nesbit, J. C., & Liu, Q. (2014). Intelligent tutoring systems and learning outcomes: A meta-analysis. *Journal of Educational Psychology, 106,* 901–918.

Mason, B. J., & Bruning, R. (2001). *Providing feedback in computer-based instruction: What the research tells us.* University of Nebraska-Lincoln. Retrieved from http://dwb.unl.edu/Edit/MB/MasonBruning.html

McClarty, K. L., Orr, A., Frey, P. M., Dolan, R. P., Vassileve, V., & McVay, A. (2012, June). *A literature review of gaming in education.* Research report. Pearson. Retrieved from http://researchnetwork.pearson.com/wp-content/uploads/Lit_Review_of_Gaming_in_Education.pdf

Meusen-Beekman, K., Joosten-ten Brinke, D., & Boshuizen, H. (2014). *The effects of formative assessment on self-regulated learning skills by sixth grade pupils*. Paper presented at EARLI, Madrid, Spain.

Mory, E. H. (2004). Feedback research revisited. In D. Jonassen (Ed.), *Handbook of research on educational communications and technology* (pp. 745–783). Mahwah, NJ: Lawrence Erlbaum.

Murtagh, L. (2014). The motivational paradox of feedback: Teacher and student perceptions. *Curriculum Journal, 25,* 516–541.

Pajares, F., & Graham, L. (1998). Formalist thinking and language arts instruction: Teachers' and students' beliefs about truth and caring in the teaching conversation. *Teaching and Teacher Education, 14,* 855–870.

Panadero, E. (2016). Social, interpersonal and human effects of assessing my peers: A review and future directions. In G. T. L. Brown & L. Harris (Eds.), *Human factors and social conditions of assessment* (pp. 247–266). London: Routledge.

Panadero, E., Tapia, J. A., & Huertas, J. A. (2012). Rubrics and self-assessment scripts effects on self-regulation, learning and self-efficacy in secondary education. *Learning and Individual Differences, 22*(6), 806–813. doi:10.1016/j.lindif.2012.04.007

Peterson, E. R., & Irving, S. E. (2008). Secondary school students' conceptions of assessment and feedback. *Learning and Instruction, 18,* 238–250.

Pintrich, P. R., & Zusho, A. (2002). The development of academic self-regulation: The role of cognitive and motivational factors. In A. Wigfield & J. S. Eccles (Eds.), *Development of achievement motivation* (pp. 249–284). San Diego: Academic Press.

Pokorny, H., & Pickford, P. (2010). Complexity, cues, and relationships: Student perceptions of feedback. *Active Learning in Higher Education, 11,* 21–30.

Ross, J. A. (2006). The reliability, validity, and utility of self-assessment. *Practice Assessment Research and Evaluation, 11*(10).

Sebba, J., Deakin Crick, R., Yu, G., Lawson, H., Harlen, W., & Durant, K. (2008, October). *Systematic review of research evidence of the impact on students in secondary schools of self and peer assessment* (EPPI-Centre Social Science Research Unit Report No. 1614). London: Institute of Education, University of London.

Surendeleg, G., Murwa, V., Yun, H.-K., & Kim, Y. S. (2014). The role of gamification in education—A literature review. *Contemporary Engineering Sciences, 7,* 1609–1616.

Topping, K. J. (2013). Peers as a source of formative and summative assessment. In J. H. McMillan (Ed.), *Sage handbook of research on classroom assessment* (pp. 395–412). Los Angeles: Sage.

Van der Kleij, F. M., Feskens, R. C. W., & Eggen, T. J. H. M. (2015). Effects of feedback in a computer-based learning environment on students' learning outcomes: A meta-analysis. *Review of Educational Research, 85*(4), 475–511.

Weaver, M. R. (2006). Do students value feedback? Student perceptions of tutors' written responses. *Assessment and Evaluation in Higher Education, 31,* 379–394.

Wiliam, D. (2011). *Embedded formative assessment.* Bloomington, IN: Solution Tree Press.

Wylie, E. C., & Lyon, C. J. (2015). The fidelity of formative assessment implementation: Issues of breadth and quality. *Assessment in Education: Principles, Policy and Practice, 22,* 140–160.

Zimmerman, B., & Schunk, D. (Eds.). (2011). *Handbook of self-regulation of learning and performances.* New York, NY: Routledge.

6

Improving Classroom Feedback

In this book, we have insisted that what matters most about feedback is that students use it. And feedback must make sense to students if they are to use it. Effective feedback should improve students' learning, and even better, it should improve students' ability to approach new tasks.

To make the use of feedback a routine part of students' learning, you must intentionally build feedback episodes into your instructional planning. Formative assessment cycles should be built into all unit and lesson plans. The first part of this chapter focuses on proactively planning feedback episodes into a unit. The second part focuses on what we considered was the "take away" from the book. We approach the discussion of the take away as questions that you may ask about feedback.

Proactively Planning Feedback Episodes

There is no magic formula for predicting all the opportunities that students will provide for you to implement feedback episodes. However, you still can look for opportunities, some formal (e.g., a test), some less than formal (e.g., an exit ticket), and some informal (e.g., one-to-one conversations with students). Our discussion of building feedback episodes proactively builds on the concept of three types of curricula (Schmidt et al., 1996): *intended curriculum*—refers to the content, pedagogy, and structure expressed in the instructional materials that reflect the developers' theory of knowledge and skill acquisition; *implemented curriculum*—refers to the way teachers deliver the instructional materials; and *learned (attained) curriculum*—refers to what students experience and integrate in their existing knowledge and skill structure. For the purpose of our discussion, *curriculum* should be understood as the unit or the module or the chapter or the topic that is the focus of the instruction.

Understanding the Intended Curriculum With Feedback Episodes in Mind

To implement assessment for learning with your students, you should first be familiar with the big idea at the center of the unit you will teach. You need to keep in mind the "scheme of *progression*" (Black, Wilson, & Yao, 2011, p. 74) underlying the big idea of the unit. You need to understand first, the intended curriculum. More specifically, this means understanding the particular knowledge and skills to be taught and learned during the unit, according to how the unit is designed. This instructional awareness is essential because of the strong links between the characteristics of the unit (or the curriculum), and the characteristics of instruction and assessment. There are several reasons that understanding the unit is relevant for feedback episodes. Understanding the unit:

1. clarifies what the learning goals of the unit are—the "bottom line" of what students need to learn;
2. helps you understand the opportunities provided (or missed) for students to achieve those learning goals and organize the instruction accordingly (e.g., by supplementing the unit with other learning opportunities);

3. helps you decide where the critical junctures in the unit are where you will formally collect information from all the students;

4. makes evident how students' thinking becomes more sophisticated as the unit unfolds;

5. guides you on the aspects of students' learning on which they need to focus;

6. helps you decide on the characteristics of the instructional tasks that are aligned to the learning goals and can support students' learning, and

7. helps you to proactively build feedback episodes.

Understanding the unit provides a *framework* for you to determine where formal formative assessment (FFA) can be embedded, and it helps you to align "students' developing ideas and methods with the disciplinary ideas that they ultimately are accountable for knowing" (e.g., Stein, Engle, Smith, & Hughes, 2008, p. 319).

Some criteria for identifying the natural junctures of a unit to build formal formative feedback episodes are (a) a sub-goal of the end-of-unit goal is achieved—there is a body of knowledge and skills sufficiently comprehensive to be assessed, and (b) you need to know about students' understanding before they proceed with further instruction (Ayala et al., 2008). Feedback to students in these junctures is critical to help them improve their understanding and skills of the material already taught, before instruction continues.

Having a framework of the unit will also help you to better facilitate student conversations during informal formative assessment (IFA) episodes because you will more effectively recognize students' critical ideas during oral dialogues at either the individual level or during whole-class interactions. The framework serves as a mental reminder to make sure that the important disciplinary ideas are being developed as the unit is being implemented. It can also help locate students' conceptions along the trajectory, which in turn offer guidance about what to do next with the student—what questions to ask or what activities to conduct to help the student move forward.

Implementing a Unit Framed by Feedback Episodes

We have emphasized that most things that students say, do, write, and make are sources of information about their understanding and, therefore, potential sources of meaningful feedback. We also have emphasized the importance of whole-class discussions and one-to-one dialogues as powerful tools for enhancing student learning (Alexander, 2008; Cazden, 2001; Black et al., 2011), and as critical sources of formative assessment evidence.

You can proactively plan feedback episodes by leading discussions that allow students to explain, compare, challenge, and defend their claims and points of view. The *quality of the questions* asked and the *quality of tasks* in which students engage is critical to facilitating fruitful and successful discussions and interactions.

When you plan your lessons, think about valuable questions that will elicit an ample range of responses among students. Only high-quality open questions engage students in good discussions (Ruiz-Primo & Furtak, 2006, 2007). Furthermore, when you design questions that are less familiar to students and push for transfer of learning, the range of students' responses is wider (Furtak & Ruiz-Primo, 2008). Furtak and Ruiz-Primo (2008) compared students' written responses with statements they made during classroom discussions. Their results indicated that the relative success of the questions in eliciting a range of conceptions was probably due to the openness of the question and the familiarity students had with the question content. Questions with fewer constraints and unfamiliar settings elicited a range of student conceptions in writing. A comparison of written and oral questions revealed that the diversity of students' responses in writing was not reflected in oral classroom discussions. This reflects the quality of the facilitation implemented by the teachers. Classroom discussions should elicit the broad range of student thinking represented in the class, not just a few common ideas. When teachers understand unit content very well, they can lead better discussions with greater opportunity for feedback episodes.

Promoting the participation of all students is, thus, critical. "All" students includes students for whom it is difficult to express their thinking either because English is not their first language or because they have different ways of expressing what they know. Furthermore, it is important for you to listen and interpret the students' responses, and to respond to students in ways that promote discussion, summarize students' contributions, highlight contradictions, promote deeper thinking with follow-up questions, or assign students additional activities (Black et al., 2011; Ruiz-Primo & Furtak, 2006, 2007).

As has been often mentioned in this book, ensuring effective feedback depends on designing or selecting tasks that will make students' thinking explicit. Tasks should not focus just on knowing whether *students can do something*, but also on *how they do something*. This facilitates your knowledge to determine how to help them to get better (Wiliam, 2016). This is the difference between the convergent and divergent types of tasks discussed in Chapter 4 (Torrance & Pryor, 2001). Here we add that tasks should focus on those aspects identified as critical in students' learning; they should show a trajectory from less to more complex, and they should engage students in productive struggle within their learning zone: "to support engagement, instructional tasks should span multiple levels of cognitive proficiency described by the trajectory, anticipating multiple zones of proximal development among students in the classroom. This span allows all students to engage with the task despite differences in previous experiences" (Sztajn, Confrey, Wilson, & Edgington, 2012, p. 150). This means that tasks are most effective when designed with different levels of difficulty: more challenging tasks for some students, deliberate practice for others, and adapted tasks for those whose learning zones are at lower levels than their classmates.

The implementation of any unit offers students many opportunities for individual or small-group feedback episodes, in writing or in other modes. You can proactively look for feedback episodes by monitoring students' work, paying attention to the strategies students are using and to their conversations.

Understanding the Learned Unit: Summing Up the Learning With Feedback Episodes

An end-of-unit test may be formative or summative, depending on how the results of the test are used. A well-designed unit test should reflect clearly whether or not students achieve the learning goals proposed at the beginning of the unit and clearly reflect students' thinking. Unit tests typically generate a permanent record of the students' responses, which serves as a formal source of information about achievement of unit learning goals (summative). Based on this information, you can also provide helpful comments (formative) to the students individually. Moreover, you can allocate time for students to check each other's work or to self-assess their performance based on sets of assessment criteria. When quality feedback is provided by teachers and/or peers, students are empowered to take appropriate actions that lead to improved self-regulation (Andrade, 2010).

As mentioned in a previous chapter, you can also share with students how well the class as a whole performed on the unit test (e.g., share the percentage of correct responses to each question). This information shows what questions students struggle with the most, enabling discussions with teachers about how to improve. If the test questions are short-answer or essays, rather than selected-response items, you can provide a general description of what students tended to miss (e.g., "Most of your reports missed a description of the control variable; why is this information important?"). Discussing results with the whole class brings clarity about where students are and what they can do to close the gap between there and the learning goals set at the beginning of the unit—but only if more learning and assessment opportunities are presented before (or even while) going on to the next unit. Discussing results does not have to take a considerable amount of time from the class period. Follow-up actions can be taken with individuals (e.g., "Please see me at lunch"), with small groups (e.g., "I will work only with those students who have Question 5 wrong for the same reason"), or as a whole class (e.g., "Let's solve the most difficult problem as a whole class and we make sure that, as we solve the problem, we learn strategies to solve problems more than just providing the right answers").

Recapping Issues About Effective Feedback

In this section, we go over what we discussed in the previous chapters but in a succinct manner. We focus on those aspects that we believe can help improve feedback practices in your classroom. We approach the recapitulation of the book using questions.

What Is Feedback?

Feedback is information provided to students about the quality of what they think or do or make. Students then use the information to make the necessary adjustments to improve their learning. Therefore, feedback needs to be informative in order to be usable.

Who Provides Feedback?

Teachers should not be the only ones in the classroom to provide feedback. Feedback can be provided also by peers or by the students themselves if they have the necessary tools to do so (e.g., good criteria).

What Is the Best Feedback?

The best feedback is *informative* and *usable* by the student(s) who receive it. Optimal feedback indicates the difference between the current state and the desired learning state AND helps students to take a step to improve their learning. The best feedback is an instructional scaffold for the student. Feedback that is only evaluative is not effective.

What Is Effective Feedback?

Effective feedback is understandable and usable, and helps students to improve their knowledge, skills, and self-regulation habits to approach better new tasks.

Are Comments to the Students' Work the Only Form of Feedback?

In our view, feedback goes beyond written or oral comments. Formative feedback can involve any verbal exchange (conversation, dialogue, discussion, such as when a teacher responds to a student's incorrect answer with a probing question) and any instructional move (e.g., modeling, demonstrations).

How Can Students Participate in a Feedback Episode?

It is critical to involve students in the feedback process in (a) defining the evidence of learning and/or success criteria (or goal, or reference level) being targeted, (b) comparing the current or actual level of performance with the evidence or the criteria for success, and (c) using assessment information to improve their own learning to reduce the gap. A critical aspect of formative assessment is that both students and teachers participate in generating and using the assessment information. Also, students can talk with their teacher and collaboratively determine what type of feedback is more useful for them (e.g., provide examples or provide criteria or both). All of these practices entail the use of peer and self-feedback.

What Is the Focus of Feedback?

Feedback goes beyond providing comments only to students' responses to a task (e.g., a question or handout). Feedback can help students regulate their own learning and monitor their own strengths and weaknesses as reflected in their performances. This enables them to associate certain strategies with success and high-quality learning, or with unsatisfactory results. Research shows that most teachers do not adequately help students to make these associations in ways that will motive them to modify or improve unsuccessful strategies and to reinforce successful ones.

Feedback should support the meta-cognitive processes students use to learn something. We argued that feedback should also focus on the process that students used to respond and self-regulatory practices that students are using while working. Feedback can help students to improve their meta-cognitive skills and with that, their self-regulatory habits.

How One Can Think About Feedback?

Feedback is a *process* that should be considered during *each of the four formative assessment activities* in which both teachers and students are involved: *clarifying learning goals expectations or criteria, gathering information, analyzing and interpreting the information, and acting upon the information.* Feedback is strongly guided by the learning goal(s) that teacher and students are pursuing, which helps to establish expectations and criteria for success. The formative role of feedback cannot be fully understood without connecting it to the targeted learning goal and comparing the expected level with the achieved level as defined by criteria of success: Does the student's response meet the expectations (criteria)? If not, why? What evidence of student thinking is demonstrated in the response and what is needed to support the student to meet the criteria? If yes, what is the evidence in the response that the criteria was meet?

Feedback is based on the information that you collect about students. Everything that students do, write, say, or make is a source of information. Therefore, sometimes we collect information in very *informal* ways (e.g., questions, comments, observations, conversations between students) and sometimes in very *formal* ways (e.g., test or quizzes, handouts, investigation report). We can only gather the information needed to make appropriate decisions if we design or select questions or activities that help us understand how students arrive to their responses; that is, when we give students tasks that make their thinking explicit. Inappropriate or low-level questions or activities will not make students' thinking explicit. Information can be collected with different levels of formality.

Feedback is based on the interpretation that you make about the information collected from the students. Again, the learning goals, expectations, and criteria help the strategies to analyze and interpret the information collected. Just like when you gather information, analyzing and interpreting can be done very informally (i.e., on-the-fly), or very formally (e.g., calculating the percentage with which students applied the right strategy to a certain type of problem).

The most difficult activity in the four-activity cycle is to act (with a comment or an instructional move) based on the information collected and the interpretation we made about it. Both comments and instructional moves should clearly guide students on three aspects: where errors were made and how they can correct them, what processes or strategies led to those errors so students are aware of them and they can self-correct later, and self-regulation strategies that help students to learn more effectively. When feedback is directed at improving learning outcomes, its content should be focused on reducing the difference between a current understanding or performance level and what is expected. It will also seek to improve students' learning strategies, helping the students to monitor their own learning and strengthening their belief in their ability to take charge of their own learning.

How Can I Assure That Feedback Is Used and Is Useful for Students?

Ensure that your feedback is *precise* by identifying what was right or wrong in their responses and describing the ways in which something was right or wrong; *helpful* by letting the students know what to do next and what future actions to expect; and *at the right level* for the students. Furthermore, students should have an *opportunity to act on feedback* from others (teachers, peers) and plan next steps to ensure their own continued learning. When students assess themselves, they should construct their own feedback and think about how to use the information learned from self-assessment to improve their performance. Finally, students need to understand the importance of paying attention to the feedback that you, their peers, or they provide themselves. Discussing the relevance of feedback at the beginning of the school year and periodically throughout is critical.

How Can I Improve Feedback Practices to Improve Students' Learning?

Different aspects contribute to improve the quality of feedback. At the beginning of this chapter we discussed the importance of understanding the unit to look for feedback episodes. We emphasized the importance of understanding the structure and the learning goals that you and your students will need to pursue and the progression that the learning should have from one lesson to the next.

We explained the importance of developing, selecting, or adapting tasks that can help you to gather high-quality information about students' learning (i.e., tasks that make students' thinking explicit). Only with high-quality tasks can you understand where students are in their learning. We provided some questions that can help to monitor your own understanding of the unit (e.g., how does this activity contribute to the learning goal? What do students need to learn from this activity?).

We strongly suggested you proactively *anticipate* students' responses to the tasks you plan to implement, at different levels of understanding; to identify the strategies that the students may select to respond to the tasks (correct, incorrect, and partially correct); and to prepare, based on this anticipation, the different paths that you and your students will take (i.e., contingency plans). Anticipating students' responses to well-designed or carefully selected tasks is critical to building feedback episodes because it helps to anticipate the focus of the analysis and the interpretation of the students' responses (whether oral or in any other mode), and to pre-define potential paths of action. Only if you understand in advance the errors students are likely to make can you prepare in advance the specific questions and instructional moves (e.g., model strategies) to help students to be back on track. Anticipating helps you to have a framework to notice and interpret what you see, what you listen to, and how you read what students write. It gives you an *interpretative state of mind*. Still, teachers' content knowledge and pedagogical content knowledge remain a challenge, as is establishing creative classroom contexts that support, rather than constrain, students' learning.

Finally, we emphasized the importance of promoting the participation of all students. You have to engage all students in conversations and avoid focusing only on those who raise their hands. Sampling different students in different conversations makes your classroom more inclusive. It also provides you the breadth of information you need to help all students learn.

Closing Comments

This chapter focused on how to plan opportunities to maximize effective feedback episodes. It provided some strategies that should be considered in thinking about feedback episodes. It is possible to build feedback episodes into instructional planning if we have a deep understanding of the unit and know how students' learning unfolds over different lessons.

The chapter provides a summary about the characteristics of feedback that support student learning. We approached the summary as a set of questions that reflects our thinking about feedback into a framework for thinking about formative assessment that takes seriously the formative learning cycle and the active roles both students and teachers play in it. We considered the relationship between feedback and the goals of learning. We discussed characteristics of effective feedback and the interplay between feedback and the formative learning cycle. We touched on feedback from other sources besides the teacher, including student self-assessment, student peer assessment, and feedback from computers. Finally, we made suggestions for improving classroom feedback. Our approach stresses that improving feedback is not only a matter of choosing the right words or instructional moves, but also a matter of instructional planning that affords opportunities for the students to use feedback as they work their way ever closer to the goals of instruction. We invite you to apply what you have read in this book to your own teaching practice.

References

Alexander, R. (2008). *Essays on pedagogy*. New York, NY: Routledge.

Andrade, H. L. (2010). Students as the definite source of formative assessment: Academic self-assessment and the self-regulation of learning. In H. L. Andrade & G. J. Cizek (Eds.), *Handbook of formative assessment* (pp. 90–105). New York, NY: Routledge. Taylor Francis Group.

Ayala, C., Shavelson, R. J., Ruiz-Primo, M. A., Brandon, P. R., Yin, Y., Furtak, E. M., . . . Tomita, M. (2008). From formal embedded assessments to reflective lessons: The development of formative assessment studies. *Applied Measurement in Education, 21*(4), 315–334.

Black, P., Wilson, M., & Yao, S-Y. (2011). Road maps for learning: A guide to the navigation of learning progressions. *Measurement: Interdisciplinary Research and Perspectives, 9*(2–3), 71–123.

Cazden, C. B. (2001). *Classroom discourse: The language of teaching and learning.* Portsmouth, NH: Heinemann.

Furtak, E. M., & Ruiz-Primo, M. A. (2008). Making students' thinking explicit in writing and discussion: An analysis of formative assessment prompts. *Science Education, 92*(5), 799–824.

Ruiz-Primo, M. A., & Furtak, E. M. (2006). Informal formative assessment and scientific inquiry: Exploring teachers' practices and student learning. *Educational Assessment, 11*(3–4), 205–235.

Ruiz-Primo, M. A., & Furtak, E. M. (2007). Exploring teachers' informal formative assessment practices and students' understanding in the context of scientific inquiry. *Journal of Research in Science Teaching, 44*(1), 57–84.

Schmidt, W. H., Jorde, D., Cogan, L. S., Barrier, E., Gonzalo, I., Schimizu, K., . . . Wolfe, R. G. (1996). *Characterizing pedagogical flow: An investigation of mathematics and science teaching in six countries.* Dordrecht, The Netherlands: Kluwer Academic Publishers.

Stein, M. K., Engle, R. A., Smith, M. S., & Hughes, E. K. (2008). Orchestrating productive mathematical discussions: Five practices for helping teachers move beyond show and tell. *Mathematical Thinking and Learning, 10*(4), 313–340.

Sztajn, P., Confrey, J., Wilson, P. H., & Edgington, C. (2012). Learning trajectory based instruction: Toward a theory of teaching. *Educational Researcher, 41*(5), 147–156. doi:10.3102/0013189X12442801

Torrance, H., & Pryor, J. (2001). Developing formative assessment in the classroom: Using action to explore and modify theory. *British Educational Research Journal, 27*(5), 615–631.

Wiliam, D. (2016). The secret of effective feedback. *Educational Leadership, 73*(7), 10–15.

Index

Boldface page references indicate tables. *Italic* references indicate figures.

 Taylor & Francis eBooks

---

Helping you to choose the right eBooks for your Library

Add Routledge titles to your library's digital collection today. Taylor and Francis ebooks contains over 50,000 titles in the Humanities, Social Sciences, Behavioural Sciences, Built Environment and Law.

Choose from a range of subject packages or create your own!

Benefits for you
» Free MARC records
» COUNTER-compliant usage statistics
» Flexible purchase and pricing options
» All titles DRM-free.

Benefits for your user
» Off-site, anytime access via Athens or referring URL
» Print or copy pages or chapters
» Full content search
» Bookmark, highlight and annotate text
» Access to thousands of pages of quality research at the click of a button.

eCollections – Choose from over 30 subject eCollections, including:

Archaeology	Language Learning
Architecture	Law
Asian Studies	Literature
Business & Management	Media & Communication
Classical Studies	Middle East Studies
Construction	Music
Creative & Media Arts	Philosophy
Criminology & Criminal Justice	Planning
Economics	Politics
Education	Psychology & Mental Health
Energy	Religion
Engineering	Security
English Language & Linguistics	Social Work
Environment & Sustainability	Sociology
Geography	Sport
Health Studies	Theatre & Performance
History	Tourism, Hospitality & Events

For more information, pricing enquiries or to order a free trial, please contact your local sales team:
www.tandfebooks.com/page/sales

Printed in the USA
CPSIA information can be obtained
at www.ICGtesting.com
LVHW052003140923
758260LV00010B/333

9 781138 646575